# AUSTRIA

## SKI GUIDE

D0434309

**By Steve Pooley**
and the Staff of Berlitz Guides

**Series Editor:** Christina Jackson

**Assistant Editor:** Amanda Hopkins

**Editorial Assistant:** Felicitas Krause

**Design:** Dominique Michellod

**Layout:** Doris Haldemann

**Vignettes:** Max Thommen

**Photography:** cover, pp. 23, 26 Achenkirch Tourist Office; skier insert, 13, 114, 116, 117 Lech Tourist Office; pp. 2–3, 105, 106 Kirchberg Tourist Office; pp. 33, 39, 40, 44, 63, 79, 87, 95, 109, 130, 131, 163, 171, 174, 206, 208, 211 Jürg Donatsch; pp. 10, 30 Alpbach Tourist Office; pp. 11, 65, 69 Filzmoos Tourist Office; pp. 14, 17, 51 Bad Kleinkirchheim Tourist Office; pp. 19, 45 Vorauer, Bad Hofgastein Tourist Office; p. 55 Brand Tourist Office; p. 58 Ellmau Tourist Office; p. 62 Fieberbrunn Tourist Office; p. 74 Fügen Tourist Office; pp. 84–85 Lanersbach Tourist Office; p. 102 Ischgl Tourist Office; p. 124 Lermoos Tourist Office; p. 125 Mayrhofen Tourist Office; p. 136 Niederau Tourist Office; p. 141 Obergurgl Tourist Office; pp. 144, 146, 151 Saalbach Tourist Office; pp. 157, 150 St. Anton Tourist Office; pp. 165, 169 St. Johann in Tirol Tourist Office; p. 180 Schruns Tourist Office; p. 187 Seefeld Tourist Office; pp. 189, 192 Serfaus Tourist Office; pp. 198, 199 Sölden Tourist Office; p. 200 Söll Tourist Office; p. 217 Zell am See Tourist Office; pp. 224–225 Zürs Tourist Office.

## Acknowledgments

We wish to thank all the local and regional tourist offices, as well as the Austrian National Tourist Office in London, in particular Barbara Gruel, for providing information, maps and photos, and ADAC Verlag GmbH, for allowing us access to the films of their piste maps. We are also grateful to Jay Dowle for his help in the preparation of this guide and to Austrian Airlines and the Ski Club of Great Britain for assistance.

Cover photo: Achenkirch; pp. 2–3 Kirchberg.

# CONTENTS

**Maps**

West Austria 7; East Austria 8; Achenkirch 24–25; Alpbach 29; Radstadter Tauern 34–35; Gasteinertal 42–43; Bad Kleinkirchheim 48–49; Brand 53; Fieberbrunn 61; Filzmoos/Neuberg 66–67; Fügen 72–73; Galtür/Silvretta 76–77; Tuxertal 82–83; Hochkönig 88–89; Innsbruck 92–93; Ischgl/Silvretta 98–99; Kitzbühel Ski Region 110–111; Lech/Zürs 118–119; Lermoos 123; Stubaital 133; Niederau 135; Saalbach-Hinterglemm 148–149; Ski Arlberg 154–155; St. Johann im Pongau 161; St. Johann in Tirol 166–167; Schladming 172–173; Montafon 178–179; Seefeld 184–185; Serfaus 190–191; Ötztal Arena 196–197; Wilder Kaiser-Brixental 202–203; Zell am See/Kaprun 214–215; Zell am Ziller 220–221.

*Although we make every effort to ensure the accuracy of all the information in this book, changes occur incessantly. We cannot therefore take responsibility for facts, addresses and circumstances in general that are constantly subject to alteration.*

*All ratings of resorts in this guide were made without bias, partiality or prejudice and reflect the author's own subjective opinion. The information on the facts and figures pages was supplied by the resorts themselves. Prices shown are the most up to date available from the resort at the time of going to press. They should, however, only be taken as an indication of what to expect.*

**WEST AUSTRIA**

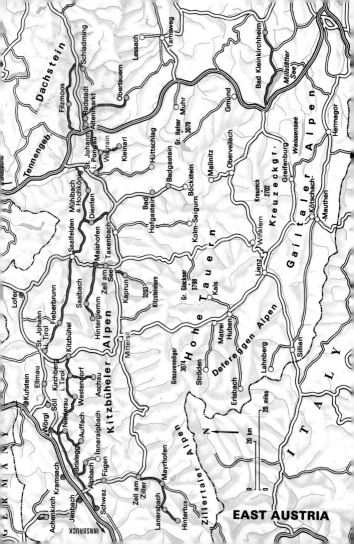

**EAST AUSTRIA**

# AUSTRIA AND ITS SKIING

For winter sports enthusiasts, Austria is synonymous with skiing. There are few of the high-altitude, purpose-built resorts to rival those in France but, instead, you'll find a charming welcome, traditional methods of tuition and an invariably high standard of accommodation.

The essence of Austria's skiing is not in the bald statistics poured out by the tourist office: 21,000 km. of runs, 9,500 ski lifts of various types, 8,500 instructors... though these are certainly formidable. What draws visitors back year after year is the chance to enjoy top-class skiing in an atmosphere of *Gemütlich-keit*—that elusive combination of cosy charm and friendliness that permeates many Austrian resorts. The world's image of the typical Austrian ski *Dorf* of painted stucco and wood chalets clustered round an onion-domed church is no fairy-tale creation. Most of them really *are* like that.

Austria is particularly good for groups of mixed ability, even including non-skiers. If you are looking for an all-round winter sports holiday, you'll find a whole range of après-ski and non-skiing activities. Most resorts have cleared paths for walking, skating and curling rinks. Many have indoor swimming pools and tennis courts, while the better hotels have their own pools, sauna, steam room, solarium and massage facilities.

Most tour operators organize a host of evening activities. A typical week's programme will include bowling, tobogganing, sleigh-rides, an "Austrian evening" (which can vary from traditional entertainment to downright stupid party games fuelled by copious quantities of beer and schnapps) and a fondue supper.

Excursions for non-skiers are usually available, the most popular being to two of Austria's most exquisite cities, Innsbruck and Salzburg, and over the Brenner Pass to the South Tyrol, the region that was ceded to Italy after World War I, but is still Austrian in language and culture.

Healthy robust fare is the mainstay of Austrian cooking. The specialities that have evolved over the centuries are the result of making tasty filling meals from frugal resources for a people tackling the daily rigours of moutain life. For today's visitor, this means portions that are often too much to handle in two full meals a day. But nobody ever complains about being underfed.

Steamy mountain cabins where you can recuperate on a cold day with a bowl of *Leberknödelsuppe* (with chicken liver dumplings) or a glass of hot *Glühwein* are an essential part of skiing; on sunny days, relax on a terrace with a cold beer and a plate of *Speck* (smoked bacon) and cheese. In the Tyrol, *Gröstl* is a hearty dish of beef or pork sautéed with diced potatoes, chives, cumin and other herbs. *Wienerschnitzel*, that Viennese classic of

a large, thinly sliced cutlet of veal, coated with egg and seasoned bread crumbs and crisply sautéed, is ubiquitous.

Leave room for dessert! The national love of pastry is reflected in the variety on offer. The best-known chocolate cake is *Sachertorte*, with a layer of apricot jam. *Apfelstrudel* is thinly sliced apples with raisins and cinnamon rolled in an almost transparent flaky pastry.

To wash it all down you have a choice of white or red wines and excellent local beers, especially *Zillertaler*. The heart-warming regional firewater is, of course, schnapps.

For a dozen years, Austria has prided itself on having produced the most vivid skiing champion of all time, Franz Klammer. Now, a new batch of heroes and heroines has been spawned by the Calgary Olympics so that, suddenly, the Montafon is able to boast Anita Wachter (no less than four villages claim to be her home), while Bernard Gstrein from tiny Vent, way up a dead-end valley from Sölden and Obergurgl, has brought enormous pride to the whole Ötztaler region.

One common misconception is that Austria's skiing all takes place in the Tyrol, but from the Vorarlberg to Styria there are scores of resorts ranging from tiny ski stations with just a couple of hotels to internationally renowned centres such as St. Anton and Kitzbühel, which rank in the top echelon of anyone's list of the world's great winter sports centres.

The Vorarlberg is bordered by Switzerland, Liechtenstein, Italy and West Germany. It is largely undiscovered by British tour operators, but this has more to do with its distance from Munich and Salzburg airports, than the quality of its skiing and nightlife. Brand is a friendly little village, especially good for a relaxed holiday with children; jet-set Lech and Zürs are favoured by European royalty, as well as stars of screen and sport; the Montafon Valley, popular with the neighbouring Swiss for its reasonable prices and unstintingly high standards of comfort and efficiency, comprises five resorts all on the same lift pass.

The Arlberg network, straddling the border between Vorarlberg and Tyrol, has its own regional lift pass, which includes world-renowned St. Anton and its satellites St. Christoph and Stuben. St. Anton ranks among the greatest skiing resorts in the world and attracts a truly international clientele for peerless on-piste skiing and tough off-piste adventure. The local post bus links the entire region.

Between the Arlberg and Innsbruck, seemingly every valley running north or south from the Inn Valley has its share of skiing. The Paznaun follows the Trisanna river towards the Silvretta mountains and, after passing through See and Kappl, you reach Ischgl, a smart and lively village whose skiing terrain overlaps with that of Samnaun, a duty-free area over the Swiss border. At the head of the Paznaun valley, Galtür offers a full range of skiing, from excellent ski kindergarten to heli-skiing.

Serfaus is another upmarket village with a lot of generally easy skiing and, continuing east, the Ötztal boasts two of Austria's most popular centres, Sölden and Obergurgl. To the north, there is a clutch of small resorts, notably Lermoos, with fabulous views over the Zugspitze, and Seefeld, the great cross-country centre, also has its share of downhill skiing.

Innsbruck, capital of the Tyrol, isn't exactly a ski resort in its own right but, with mountains rising sharply on all sides, is a great base for visiting the five resorts covered by the city lift pass or branching out further afield to Seefeld or the Stubai Valley, which guarantees year-round skiing on its glacier.

The historic city is featured as an excursion option by many tour operators and travel agents. A stroll through the sedate world of the Old Town, now a pedestrian zone, will give you a glimpse into the city's past, the 15th- and 16th-century houses ornamented with colourful Baroque façades. The city's grandest monument, the Goldenes Dachl ("Little Golden Roof") was built for Emperor Maximilian I as a loggia or "royal box" from which to watch tournaments. To the east lies the cathedral, Dom zu St. Jakob, built in 1722, which stands in a tranquil square shaded by maples and copper beaches and surrounded by some of the town's oldest surviving houses. In contrast, you will see all the most modern sports installations designed for the 1964 and 1976 Olympics, which Innsbruck hosted.

Continuing east along the Inn Valley, Jenbach is at the junction of several valleys, notably the Zillertal, which contains no less than nine resorts covered by the same lift pass, such as Fügen, Zell am See and Mayrhofen, while the glacier at Hintertux is the site of summer training for the national squad.

Achenkirch, close to the Bavarian border, is the perfect place for a family holiday. Alpbach, in the next valley, has a loyal following who return year after year, seduced by the charm of one of the prettiest villages in Austria.

The Skigrossraum Wilder Kaiser-Brixental is the country's largest interlinked skiing network and is served by seven villages, notably Ellmau, Söll and Westendorf.

The Kitzbühel Alps are named after one of Austria's great ski towns, and if it is true that Kitzbühel is the best known, attracting a cosmopolitan mix of guests, the clutch of resorts in the immediate vicinity each provides a more relaxed approach. Kirchberg's skiing connects with Kitzbühel's Hahnenkamm area, scene of the most important downhill race on the world cup calendar, and the circuit continues through a linked lift system to Jochberg and thence Pass Thurn.

On the other side of the Kitzbüheler Horn, the separate resort of St. Johann in Tirol is a bustling market town. Close to the border with Salzburgerland, Fieberbrunn styles itself as the *Schneewinkl* ("Snow Pocket"), as despite being low-lying, it has a remarkable record for heavy snowfalls.

Salzburgerland features many small resorts which, linked together to form "ski circuses" or "ski shuttles", provide fast interconnecting networks for all abilities and ambitions. The biggest and best known is Saalbach-Hinterglemm, a 160-km. pisted circuit, skied in either direction with plenty of tough diversions en route.

Zell am See and Kaprun rather ambitiously style themselves as the Europa Sport Region. In addition to skiing, there are sporting opportunities a-plenty, especially in summer when the lake is a kaleidoscope of colour as windsurfers scud about in the afternoons having spent the morning skiing on the Kitzsteinhorn glacier above Kaprun.

The Gastein Valley is most famous for its spa facilities, and many visitors choose its major resorts Badgastein and Bad Hofgastein for their combination of skiing and taking the waters.

Bischofshofen is the meeting point of railways, roads and rivers, as well as being at the heart of Salzburgerland's skiing. Whilst the little market town's only sporting event takes place on the international ski jumps, it is the springboard for exploring the Hochkönig, St. Johann im Pongau and the other "3-Täler" villages, Kleinarl (home of the great Annemarie Moser-Pröll) and the rest of the Tauern Alps, including Altenmarkt, Radstadt, Zauchensee, Obertauern and Filzmoos. Between them there is everything a skier could want, because if none is particularly large, judicious use of local passes means that it is possible to ski from one valley to the next and, if accompanied by a guide, to stay well away from the crowds.

The Top-Tauern-Skischeck covers all of these resorts, as well as four over the border in Styria: Reiteralm, Rohrmoos, Haus and Schladming, the last-named a renowned World Cup centre boasting the fastest downhill course on the circuit.

The whole of Austria, quite reasonably, claims Franz Klammer as its own, but while his exploits at Innsbruck and Kitzbühel attracted the most media attention, no one can dispute Carinthia's claim to be the great man's home. Growing up on the family farm at Mooswald, he learned his skiing at Bad Kleinkirchheim and its linked resort St. Oswald.

With so much on offer, choosing a resort in Austria is not easy. But wherever you do go, you can be sure that from the grandest five-star hotel to the most modest *Gasthof*, proprietors and staff alike will be unfailingly courteous and helpful.

# HOW THE RESORTS HAVE BEEN ASSESSED

Different skiers have different requirements, and their choice of resort is influenced by many factors. In addition to the resort descriptions and facts and figures sheets, we have assessed each resort in nine categories, rating each aspect according to a mark out of ten.

**Skiing Conditions** refers to the range of skiing on offer, the quality and efficiency of the lift installations, how accessible they are and how well they interlink, whether queues are a problem and whether the resort has access to the skiing areas of other resorts. If such is the case, the extent of the other resorts' skiing will also influence the mark that it obtains.

**Snow Conditions** are governed by the height of the resort (low ones will generally have poorer snow cover at either end of the season) and its top station, whether the slopes are north- or south-facing, and whether there are snow-making facilities. Due to climatic peculiarities, some low-lying resorts enjoy heavy snowfalls and a long season. Resorts with glacier skiing usually rate highly.

The three headings **For Beginners, For Intermediates** and **For Advanced Skiers** speak for themselves. Your standard of skiing should be a major consideration when selecting a resort, as nothing is more likely to guarantee a ruined holiday than finding yourself out of your depth if a less than expert skier or being obliged to trundle round easy slopes if you are looking for something to challenge your expertise. All resorts cater in some way for beginners; however, those that have attractive, snow-sure nursery slopes or a particularly good ski school will rate more highly.

Giving the full facts about children's facilities is especially difficult. A whole book could be written about skiing with children alone; the requirements of infants, five-, ten- or fifteen-year-olds vary so enormously. Assuming that older children can be considered as adults in skiing terms, the **For Children** rating assesses a resort according to its facilities for the under-twelves, the provision of (or lack of) kindergartens both ski and non-ski, proximity of lifts and difficulty, whether there are discounts for children in ski school and on the lift pass, and if the resort is, in

general, a good place to take children. If a resort has special facilities for teenagers, it scores more highly.

For many, the **Après-Ski** is as important as the skiing. But for some, a night out can be more enjoyable in a quiet hotel restaurant than in a raucous disco into the early hours. Nonetheless, the more lively the resort, the more it will score in this category, but you should also read the text carefully to be sure that the resort features the kind of après-ski you are looking for.

Non-skiers and the energetic also look to what else is on offer in a resort. **Other Sports** covers all the non-ski activities available, but also includes cross-country skiing.

**Value for Money** does not necessarily mean low prices. The criterion here is whether the goods or services are worth the price put upon them. Some resorts are notoriously overpriced: the cost of the lift pass does not reflect the skiing available or the hotels and bars charge excessively. Other resorts may have similar prices, but you get much more for your money.

A number of Berlitz **Skiers** (from one to five) has been attributed to each resort, in the same way as hotels are given star ratings. These represent the author's overall impression and are mainly based on how extensive the skiing and facilities are. You should look to the individual ratings and the general descriptions, however, in order to assess exactly how well suited the resort is to individual needs.

# THE RESORTS AT A GLANCE

| | Altitude (metres) | Top Station (metres) | No. of Lifts | Runs (kilometres) * | Skier Rating | Skiing Conditions | Snow Conditions | For Beginners | For Intermediates | For Advanced Skiers | For Children | Après-Ski | Other Sports | Value for Money |
|---|---|---|---|---|---|---|---|---|---|---|---|---|---|---|
| Achenkirch | 930 | 1800 | 14 | 25 | 1 | 4 | 7 | 5 | 2 | 9 | 4 | 5 | 6 | 6 |
| Alpbach | 1000 | 1850 | 14 | 25 | 3 | 5 | 7 | 6 | 4 | 8 | 6 | 5 | 6 | 6 |
| Altenmarkt/Radstadt | 856 | 2188 | 37 | 100 | 1 | 3 | 5 | 8 | 2 | 6 | 3 | 4 | 5 | 5 |
| Badgastein | 870 | 2700 | 15 | 250§ | 3 | 7 | 5 | 8 | 6 | 7 | 7 | 8 | 6 | 6 |
| Bad Hofgastein | 870 | 2686 | 17 | 250§ | 3 | 7 | 5 | 8 | 6 | 6 | 7 | 8 | 6 | 6 |
| Bad Kleinkirchheim | 1100 | 2055 | 26 | 80 | 3 | 7 | 5 | 7 | 6 | 6 | 6 | 6 | 7 | 7 |
| Brand | 1050 | 1920 | 13 | 40 | 3 | 6 | 6 | 5 | 5 | 7 | 6 | 5 | 7 | 7 |
| Ellmau | 820 | 1829 | 12 | 200 | 4 | 7 | 6 | 6 | 5 | 6 | 6 | 5 | 7 | 7 |
| Fieberbrunn | 800 | 1800 | 14 | 60 | 3 | 5 | 7 | 7 | 5 | 5 | 5 | 5 | 7 | 7 |
| Filzmoos | 1057 | 2700 | 14 | 35 | 3 | 4 | 8 | 5 | 6 | 9 | 5 | 4 | 7 | 7 |
| Fügen | 545 | 2050 | 16 | 35 | 2 | 5 | 8 | 6 | 3 | 6 | 7 | 6 | 8 | 8 |
| Galtür | 1584 | 2300 | 11 | 40 | 3 | 6 | 6 | 7 | 3 | 4 | 5 | 5 | 5 | 5 |
| Hintertux/Lanersbach | 1300 | 3268 | 32 | 122 | 2 | 8 | 3 | 8 | 6 | 4 | 5 | 7 | 6 | 6 |
| Hochkönig | 854 | 1900 | 45 | 150 | 2 | 5 | 5 | 9 | 5 | 6 | 9 | 5 | 8 | 8 |
| Innsbruck | 580 | 2340 | 33 | 75 | 4 | 7 | 4 | 9 | 6 | 4 | 8 | 7 | 7 | 7 |
| Ischgl | 1400 | 2800 | 34 | 150 | 5 | 8 | 5 | 8 | 8 | 4 | 7 | 7 | 6 | 6 |
| Kirchberg | 860 | 2000 | 16 | 160 | 4 | 6 | 5 | 9 | 7 | 7 | 9 | 7 | 7 | 7 |
| Kitzbühel | 800 | 2000 | 54 | 160 | 5 | 9 | 6 | 8 | 9 | 5 | 7 | 6 | 6 | 6 |
| Lech | 1450 | 2377 | 33 | 110 | 4 | 6 | 7 | 6 | 8 | 6 | 6 | 8 | 6 | 6 |
| Lermoos | 1004 | 2118 | 7 | 22 | 3 | 6 | 8 | 6 | 3 | 6 | 5 | 7 | 6 | 6 |

| Resort | | | | | | | | | | | | | | |
|---|---|---|---|---|---|---|---|---|---|---|---|---|---|---|
| Mayrhofen | 630 | 2250 | 29 | 90 | 3 | 5 | 5 | 7 | 7 | 2 | 7 | 7 | 7 | 5 | 7 |
| Neustift/Stubai Valley | 1000 | 3200 | 42 | 120 | 3 | 5 | 8 | 5 | 5 | 5 | 5 | 5 | 5 | 7 | 7 |
| Niederau | 828 | 1903 | 12 | 40§ | 3 | 5 | 6 | 8 | 8 | 4 | 8 | 5 | 5 | 5 | 7 |
| Obergurgl | 1930 | 3082 | 21 | 100§ | 3 | 6 | 7 | 8 | 8 | 5 | 7 | 5 | 5 | 5 | 6 |
| Obertauern | 1740 | 2350 | 27 | 90 | 3 | 8 | 7 | 6 | 8 | 6 | 5 | 6 | 6 | 5 | 6 |
| Saalbach-Hinterglemm | 1003 | 2097 | 57 | 180 | 5 | 9 | 7 | 5 | 5 | 8 | 5 | 9 | 6 | 6 | 6 |
| St. Anton | 1304 | 2650 | 42 | 300§ | 5 | 10 | 8 | 4 | 4 | 10 | 5 | 9 | 6 | 6 | 6 |
| St. Johann im Pongau | 650 | 1850 | 17 | 105 | 3 | 7 | 6 | 6 | 6 | 5 | 5 | 5 | 6 | 6 | 8 |
| St. Johann in Tirol | 660 | 1700 | 18 | 50 | 3 | 6 | 6 | 6 | 6 | 5 | 5 | 7 | 6 | 6 | 8 |
| Schladming | 745 | 2015 | 24 | 60 | 4 | 7 | 6 | 5 | 6 | 6 | 6 | 8 | 8 | 8 | 8 |
| Schruns/Montafon | 700 | 2400 | 73 | 206 | 3 | 4 | 6 | 6 | 8 | 6 | 7 | 8 | 8 | 7 | 8 |
| Seefeld | 1200 | 2074 | 17 | 25 | 3 | 5 | 6 | 7 | 6 | 3 | 6 | 7 | 8 | 5 | 7 |
| Serfaus | 1427 | 2745 | 19 | 40 | 2 | 5 | 6 | 6 | 7 | 3 | 6 | 6 | 8 | 7 | 5 |
| Sölden | 1377 | 3058 | 33 | 101 | 4 | 8 | 9 | 5 | 8 | 7 | 5 | 7 | 8 | 5 | 7 |
| Söll | 703 | 1829 | 13 | 200§ | 4 | 8 | 8 | 8 | 9 | 5 | 6 | 7 | 6 | 8 | 8 |
| Westendorf | 800 | 2000 | 14 | 200 | 2 | 5 | 5 | 8 | 5 | 2 | 8 | 8 | 5 | 8 | 8 |
| Zauchensee/Kleinarl | 1014 | 1980 | 36 | 80 | 1 | 5 | 5 | 4 | 6 | 2 | 4 | 4 | 5 | 5 | 5 |
| Zell am See/Kaprun | 750 | 3029 | 51 | 125 | 3 | 7 | 8 | 5 | 8 | 4 | 5 | 6 | 7 | 7 | 5 |
| Zell am Ziller | 580 | 2240 | 24 | 42 | 3 | 6 | 6 | 7 | 6 | 3 | 6 | 6 | 6 | 6 | 6 |
| Zürs | 1720 | 2850 | 10 | 110 | 4 | 8 | 8 | 5 | 8 | 8 | 6 | 6 | 5 | 5 | 5 |

* with linked resorts
§ on same lift pass, not necessarily linked by ski

# ACHENKIRCH

Access: *Nearest airport:* Innsbruck (1 hr.); Munich (1½ hrs.). *By road:* A12 motorway, exit Achensee. *By rail:* to Jenbach, then by bus.

Tourist Office: A-6215 Achenkirch/Tyrol. Tel. (05246) 62 70

| | |
|---|---|
| Altitude: 930 m. *Top:* 1800 m. | Ski areas: Christlum, Adlerhorst |
| Language: German | Ski schools: Tiroler Schischule Achenkirch |
| Beds: 2,650 | |
| Population: 1,910 | Linked resorts: None |
| Health: Doctor and dentist in resort. *Hospital:* Schwaz (35 km.) | Season: December to April |
| Runs: 25 km. | Kindergarten: *Non-ski:* in hotel. *With ski:* from 3½ years. |
| Lifts: 14 | |

Prices: *Lift pass:* 6 days 910 S. *Ski school:* Group 950 S for 6 days; private 320 S per hour.

# RATINGS

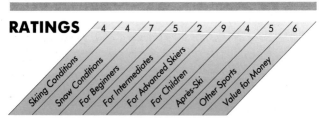

| Skiing Conditions | Snow Conditions | For Beginners | For Intermediates | For Advanced Skiers | For Children | Après-Ski | Other Sports | Value for Money |
|---|---|---|---|---|---|---|---|---|
| 4 | 4 | 7 | 5 | 2 | 9 | 4 | 5 | 6 |

# THE RESORT

Just over an hour's drive from Munich, Achenkirch is usually bypassed by keen Bavarian skiers who flood over the border to visit bigger Tyrolean centres. The village is a dispersed settlement at the tip of the Achensee lake—a great sailing and wind-surfing centre in summer. It is best suited to families and unambitious couples who enjoy a friendly atmosphere and gorgeous views over the frozen lake.

# THE SKIING

The upper part of the Christlum mountain is a wide bowl, steep in the centre and gentle on the flanks, meaning that a descent can be either as easy or difficult as required; the lower section is tree-lined and, generally, easy. There are few perils on the 25 km. of marked trails.

The ski school has a high reputation for the instruction and care of children, and experts can enrol in the ski school's top class,

which provides a week's slalom sessions, touring tuition and off-piste practice. English is spoken, with a hint of an Australian twang, since several of the instructors spend their summers "down under".

Every Friday, there is an all-comers' race under WiSBI rules, Austria's national handicap scheme. For further variety, Maurach and Pertisau are easily reached by the local bus service, each providing a good day's excursion.

# APRÈS-SKI

For immediately after skiing, there is a little bar at the end of the slopes down from the Christlumalm mid-station restaurant, where parents rendezvous with their offspring after ski classes or tobogganing. The atmosphere of the village is low-key, but there is dancing in the Ossi, Achenseer Tenne, Achentalerhof and Posthotel.

# OTHER ACTIVITIES

There are more than 50 km. of marked trails for cross-country skiing and a further 20 km. for walking. Children love the toboggan run on the Christlum, and the Tiroler Adler and Almgasthof both have "skittle nooks". Guests at the grandest hotel in the area, the Posthotel, have horse riding and indoor tennis at their disposal, as well as a sauna, Jacuzzi, Turkish bath and swimming pool, plus health treatments using Tyrolean "rock oil" to combat rheumatic complaints.

The attractive town of Innsbruck is 50 km. away, and a visit is feasible by driving or taking a bus to Jenbach and thence the main-line railway.

# ALPBACH

Access: *Nearest airport:* Innsbruck (1 hr.); Munich (2 hrs.). *By road:* A12 motorway, exit Kramsach. *By rail:* to Brixlegg, then by bus.

Tourist Office: A-6236 Alpbach. Tel. (05336) 52 11

Altitude: 1000 m. *Top:* 1850 m.

Language: German

Beds: 2,400

Population: 2,000

Health: Doctor in resort. *Hospital:* Wörgl (25 km.)

Runs: 25 km.

Lifts: 14

Ski areas: Inneralpbach, Greiter Graben

Ski schools: Alpbacher Schischule

Linked resorts: None

Season: Mid-December to Easter

Kindergarten: *Non-ski:* from 3 years. *With ski:* from 4 years.

Prices: *Lift pass:* 6 days 950–990 S (children 640–670 S). *Ski school:* Group 950 S for 6 days; private 320 S per hour.

# RATINGS

| Skiing Conditions | Snow Conditions | For Beginners | For Intermediates | For Advanced Skiers | For Children | Après-Ski | Other Sports | Value for Money |
|---|---|---|---|---|---|---|---|---|
| 5 | 5 | 7 | 6 | 4 | 8 | 6 | 5 | 6 |

# THE RESORT

Alpbach embodies Alpine charm, and its timeless Tyrolean atmosphere attracts a discerning and predominantly monied clientele who return year after year. Situated above the valley which lies between the Wildschönau and the Zillertal, Alpbach is an ancient settlement with a history dating back over 2,500 years and boasts inns such as the Böglerhof and Jakober which were established in 1470 and 1608 respectively. Before 1926 there was only a small track from Brixlegg (in the Inn valley between Wörgl and Jenbach) to Alpbach, ensuring that local customs and traditions had become deep-rooted. As the resort gained in popularity, however, rather than leaping into modernity, the village fathers chose to impose strict guidelines for new construction so that the old rustic atmosphere has not been lost. Nonetheless, inside the several classy hotels there are airy dining rooms, bars stocked with an international array of drinks, and ultra-modern health facilities—the wood-panelled *Stuberls* have been carefully preserved, of course.

A poll conducted on Austrian television voted Alpbach the country's prettiest village and, with so many gorgeous settlements in Austria, this accolade should be taken seriously. The affection with which Alpbach is held has little to do with its ski slopes, which for all their prettiness and occasional challenging sections are limited in scope, but is due to its being *the* archetypal Tyrolean ski *Dorf*. Older instructors enjoy teaching the children of visitors who first learned in Alpbach 30 years ago, and it is quite common for families of three generations to travel here together.

# THE SKIING

Strict maintenance of the old architectural style in the village hasn't precluded development on the mountain. The recently installed chair lifts from Inneralpbach, a separate village five minutes away, and the Gmahbahn triple chair have both improved uphill capacity and comfort and are to be complemented by a new gondola from Achenwirt to just above the Hornboden restaurant for the 1988/89 season. New lifts straddling the Standkopf (2228 m.) will open a completely new area, but this is as yet only planned.

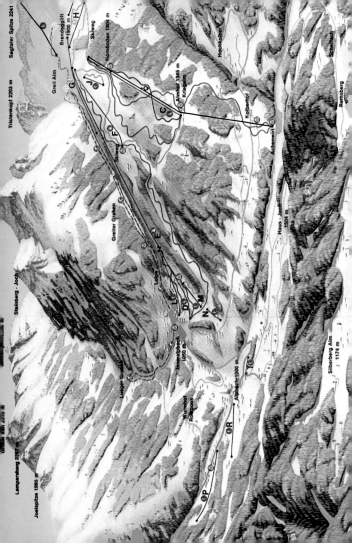

The conical mountain's upper reaches are wide open, meaning that descents can be as steep or gentle as required, and there are several long trails lower down, including the Schoberried run which is used for FIS races and is the occasional venue for the British Junior Championships. The drawback is that it is necessary to drive or use the free bus service for access. Beginners, however, start on nursery slopes at the edge of the village. The lift pass also includes Reith, a smaller resort back down the valley towards Brixlegg.

# APRÈS-SKI

As you would expect, après-ski activities are thoroughly traditional, although there are two discos to satisfy young spirits. The large bar in the Böglerhof, which is frequently the scene of musical evenings, is the most popular gathering place at the end of the day and, ten minutes walk from the centre of the village, the Hotel Alphof's nightclub stages both Tyrolean evenings and disco nights.

The ski school's prize-giving party takes place on Friday evenings, live bands occasionally appear in the larger hotels, and sleigh-ride parties to the Rossmoos for music and dancing are organized by tour operators.

# OTHER ACTIVITIES

For a village of its size, Alpbach boasts an excellent indoor swimming pool with adjacent natural facilities for skating and curling. Tyrolean skittles evenings are organized, and toboggans can be hired for a small daily charge. Cross-country skiing tuition, as well as equipment hire, is available, and there are extensive *Loipen* further up the valley beyond Inneralpbach.

The more sedate pleasure of walking is particularly well serviced. Josef Daxer's *Wandern im Alpbach* outlines over a hundred walks and mountain hikes and, along with a walker's map, is available from the tourist office opposite the church. Many itineraries conveniently suggest refuelling stops at tiny mountain *Hütten*.

Alpbach is very much getting away from it all territory, but if you venture down to the Inn valley by car or post bus, the glass factory at Rattenberg, which is also available on excursions, provides the opportunity to observe the fascinating craftsmanship and buy custom-made souvenirs. Brixlegg is on the main line between Kufstein and Innsbruck, each of them well worth visiting for a taste of ancient urban Tyrol, and excursions are possible to Salzburg, Aurach's wildlife park, Kitzbühel, Innsbruck and Italy's South Tyrol. Closer to hand, the Farmhouse Museum in Inneralpbach (open on Wednesdays) is a testament to the valley's rural history.

# ALTENMARKT/ RADSTADT

Access: *Nearest airport:* Salzburg (45 mins.). *By road:* A10 motorway, exit Eben. *By rail:* railway station in Radstadt, bus to Altenmarkt.

Tourist Office: A-5541 Altenmarkt. Tel. (06452) 74 61

Altitude: 856 m. *Top:* 1770 m.

Language: German

Beds: 3,890 in Altenmarkt, 4,000 in Radstadt

Population: 4,000 Radstadt, 2,894 Altenmarkt

Health: Doctor in both resorts. *Hospital:* Schwarzach (30 km.)

Runs: 100 km. with Zauchensee-Kleinarl

Lifts: 37 (320 on Top-Tauern-Skischeck)

Ski areas: Radstadt, Altenmarkt

Ski schools: Schischule Radstadt, Schischule Altenmarkt und Zauchensee

Linked resorts: Kleinarl, St. Johann, Flachau, Wagrain, Zauchensee, Flachauwinkl

Season: December to April

Kindergarten: *Non-ski:* from 3 years. *With ski:* from 4 years.

Prices: *Lift pass:* 6 days 1160 S (children 710 S). *Ski school:* Group 930 S for 6 days; private 380 S per hour.

# RATINGS

| Skiing Conditions | Snow Conditions | For Beginners | For Intermediates | For Advanced Skiers | For Children | Après-Ski | Other Sports | Value for Money |
|---|---|---|---|---|---|---|---|---|
| 3 | 4 | 5 | 3 | 2 | 5 | 3 | 4 | 5 |

# THE RESORTS

Largely undiscovered by tour operators, Altenmarkt and Radstadt are just off the Salzburg-Villach *Autobahn*. Each has a small skiing area which combined provides a good variety of easy intermediate slopes as well as nursery areas. Either is an excellent base from which to explore the district which straddles the border between Salzburgerland and Styria and which has its own regional lift pass, the Top-Tauern-Skischeck. All make pleasant day excursions but you will need your own transport if travelling independently.

Radstadt is the larger of the two resorts and therefore livelier, whilst Altenmarkt is prettier and has a particularly helpful tourist office which can assist independent travellers with accommodation enquiries.

H. Galsstein 2192 m

OBE

Grunwaldkopf

Fageralmen

Gnade

Seitenalm

UNTERTAUERN

Löbenau

Tauernloipe

RADSTADT

1597 m

Roßbrand 1770 m

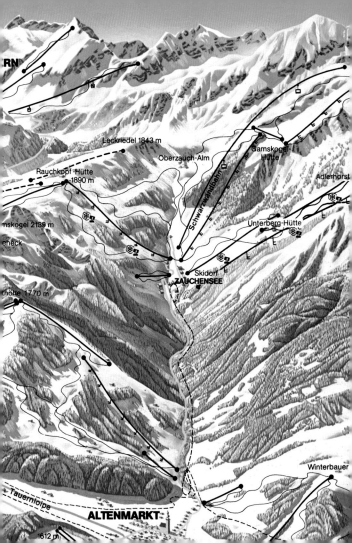

# THE SKIING

The few operators which feature Altenmarkt or Radstadt organize transport by coach every day to the local areas or further afield. If you are content to confine activities to the immediate vicinity, the post bus runs an efficient service which takes you up the valley, past Altenmarkt's lifts, to Zauchensee and thence to Kleinarl via Flachauwinkl, where the *Autobahn* is crossed by the Winkl Express—a couple of open carriages hauled by a tractor disguised as a steam locomotive! A competent skier can make it to Kleinarl and back in a day, and most choose to take lunch at the café owned and run by Austria's great ladies' downhill champion, Annemarie Moser-Pröll.

With the Kemathöhe top station at just 1770 m., the two resorts have a relatively short season, so it is best to check snow conditions if planning to visit before mid-January or after the middle of March.

There are a few off-piste opportunities for experts, but the Altenmarkt-Radstadt area is best for easy cruising or to visit when exploring the Tauern mountains.

# APRÈS-SKI

Evening activities are low-key and informal, and neither town should be considered by anyone looking for glittering nightclubs or celebrity-spotting. There are plenty of pleasant restaurants and a few lively, unpretentious discos (the Tauernstuben and Archnoah) and *Tanzcafés* ("dance cafés").

# OTHER ACTIVITIES

The 50-km. Tauernloipe network of cross-country trails links Altenmarkt and Radstadt with Eben, Wagrain and Flachau and is easily accessible from both towns, with several shorter trails nearby. There is a public swimming pool and another four in hotels, plus indoor tennis.

A visit to the Atomic ski factory in Altenmarkt can be arranged. The railway line runs along the Enns valley to Schladming and then on to Salzburg—an elegant and sophisticated diversion from skiing.

# BADGASTEIN

Access: *Nearest airport:* Salzburg (1½ hr.); Munich (3 hrs.). *By road:* A10 motorway, exit Bischofshofen. *By rail:* railway station in Badgastein.

Tourist Office: A-5640 Badgastein. Tel. (06434) 25 31

Altitude: 870 m. *Top:* 2686 m.

Language: German

Beds: 7,700

Population: 5,600

Health: Doctors and clinic, famous spa in resort.
*Hospital:* Schwarzach (25 km.)

Runs: 80 km. (250 km. in Gasteinertal)

Lifts: 15 (50 in Gasteinertal)

Ski areas: Stubnerkogel, Graukogel

Ski schools: Schischule Badgastein

Linked resorts: Bad Hofgastein

Season: December to May

Kindergarten: *Non-ski:* from 2½ years. *With ski:* from 3 years.

Prices: *Lift pass:* 1,190–1,400 S (children 850 S). *Ski school:* Group 1150 S for 6 days; private 380 S per hour.

# RATINGS

| Skiing Conditions | Snow Conditions | For Beginners | For Intermediates | For Advanced Skiers | For Children | Après-Ski | Other Sports | Value for Money |
|---|---|---|---|---|---|---|---|---|
| 7 | 7 | 5 | 8 | 6 | 6 | 7 | 8 | 6 |

*For map, see pp. 42–43.*

# THE RESORT

Badgastein is the best known of the quartet of Gasteinertal resorts Dorfgastein, Bad Hofgastein and Sportgastein (the last being no more than a ski station without accommodation).

As the name suggests, Badgastein has a well-established reputation as a spa town. It is grander than most Austrian resorts, the architecture a departure from the Alpine stereotype of quaint chalets and wooden, galleried barns. Instead, grandiose hotels loom above the Ache river, and swimming in thermal baths or taking the *Kur* are more popular than disco dancing. The young set, therefore, tends to choose livelier places for a winter holiday, but the skiing above the valley is far from sedate—the best endorsement is that it is one of the most popular resorts for Austrians.

# THE SKIING

The area pass, which includes Dorfgastein, Bad Hofgastein and Sportgastein, covers 55 lifts and 250 km. of well-maintained piste and, as well as attracting contestants for World Cup races, provides all grades of recreational skiers with plenty of variety and challenge.

Far from resting on its considerable laurels, the area has made a huge investment in maintaining and developing the lift systems, notably the installation of the aerodynamically designed two-stage gondola from the village to the Stubnerkogel (2246 m.). Its construction is such that there is minimal agitation in high wind. From the top, there is an 11-km. intermediate run to the Skizentrum Angertal, which is the connecting point between Badgastein and Bad Hofgastein. Should you lose track of time at the end of the day and find that the lifts have closed, there are ski buses back to both villages.

The Hüttenkogel (2231 m.), on the opposite side of the valley and start of the World Cup courses, is the highest point, although Sportgastein has a top station at 2686 m. On sunny days, there is glorious skiing above the tree line with equally glorious views across, and down, the valley. If the weather closes in, the trees on the lower slopes aid visibility and give protection against high winds. The main part of the skiing is on mountain pastures, which are almost entirely rock-free, so that skiing is possible with the lightest snow cover—an important consideration at the beginning or end of the season.

The Gastein Superski lift pass facilitates use of buses and trains between the valley's various ski centres. Should you be exploring the region by car over a period of several weeks, the Golden Skicard is a season pass which covers the Gasteinertal, Grossarl, Kaprun and Zell am See, Schladming and the rest of the Dachstein-Tauern region, Obertauern and Franz Klammer's home slopes at Bad Kleinkirchheim.

## APRÈS-SKI

The Metropolis and Muhlhäusl discos play throbbing music until the small hours, but dancing to small bands in the Hotel Bellevue is more in keeping with Badgastein's image. Or you can join the high rollers in the casino; Badgastein optimistically styles itself the "Monte Carlo of the Alps".

## OTHER ACTIVITIES

Just about the full gamut of sporting activities is available: swimming in indoor and outdoor thermally heated pools, indoor tennis and horse riding, squash, bowling, skating, curling, skibob, and walking along 35 km. of cleared paths, plus some 80 km. of cross-country trails around the valley.

In addition to taking the waters, you can visit the local history museum, or indulge in some shopping. For trips out of town, Badgastein is on the main railway line between Salzburg and Villach.

# BAD HOFGASTEIN

Access: *Nearest airport:* Salzburg (1 hr.). *By road:* A10 motorway, exit Bischofshofen, then via Salzachtal. *By rail:* to Badgastein, then by bus.

Tourist Office: A-5630 Bad Hofgastein. Tel. (06432) 64 81

Altitude: 870 m. *Top:* 2686 m.

Language: German

Beds: 8,900 in hotels, 2,500 in chalets and apartments

Population: 5,940

Health: Doctors in resort. *Hospital:* Schwarzach (25 km.)

Runs: 75 km. (250 km. in Gasteinertal)

Lifts: 17 (50 in Gasteinertal)

Ski areas: Kitzstein, Schlossalm, Hohe Scharte, Angertal

Ski schools: Schischule Bad Hofgastein

Linked resorts: Badgastein

Season: December to May

Kindergarten: *Non-ski:* from 3 years. *With ski:* from 3 years.

Prices: *Lift pass:* 6 days 1,400 S (children 850 S). *Ski school:* Group 950 S for 6 days; private 380 S per hour.

# RATINGS

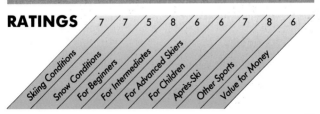

| Skiing Conditions | Snow Conditions | For Beginners | For Intermediates | For Advanced Skiers | For Children | Après-Ski | Other Sports | Value for Money |
|---|---|---|---|---|---|---|---|---|
| 7 | 7 | 5 | 8 | 6 | 6 | 7 | 8 | 6 |

# THE RESORT

Bad Hofgastein is a sturdily built town with an exquisite 15th-century church, excellent spa facilities, elegant hotels and restaurants as well as rambling, twisting alleys. A babbling brook completes the charming scenario.

The Gastein valley's thermal springs have attracted tourists since the early part of the 19th century, when they were the meeting place of the crowned heads of central Europe who congregated for the *Kur* and political debate. Today, visitors still flock here to benefit from the variety of treatments available, and tourism, apart from a little pastoral farming, is the only industry.

# THE SKIING

Even when there's minimal snow cover, skiing is still possible because most of the mountain is pastureland with very few rocks or stones. The area pass, including Badgastein, Dorfgastein and Sportgastein, covers 55 lifts and 250 km. of piste.

This is an attractive area which draws a sophisticated clientele—not necessarily monied—and prides itself on being most favoured by Austrians, resulting in a very high standard of skiing.

A funicular railway rises from the opposite side of the main road to the village and connects with a chair lift and cable car which take skiers to the large, main Schlossalm area above. The options here are to swoop down to the valley along wide, open pistes

which lead to tree-lined trails before arriving back at the bottom of the railway; or to take the Hamburger trail to the Weitmoser and Hohe Scharte lifts from where there is an 8-km. run starting just below the Hohe Scharte outcrop (2300 m.). There are some easier routes down, as well as the connection to Badgastein via Angertal.

The linking of Badgastein and Bad Hofgastein has created a very

45

large area, pretty and occasionally demanding. Should you find yourself stranded at the mid-point after the lifts have closed, there is a free ski bus home.

# APRÈS-SKI

It is easy to imagine Bad Hofgastein and its neighbours being crammed full of middle-aged people who, after a cursory examination of the slopes, indulge their rheumatic joints in the spa baths. Certainly, the therapeutic treatments of the Gastein valley attract skiers who want to cure or prevent a variety of ailments, but younger visitors looking for a lively time should not be discouraged, as there are plenty of nightclubs, bars and discos.

That being said, in common with other ski resorts which first attracted tourism through their spa facilities, the early part of the evening is often occupied with taking the waters in one form or another—a thoroughly relaxing interlude between skiing and a pre-dinner drink. Eating out is invariably a pleasant experience whether at a little café tucked away in an alley or at somewhere grand such as the Weitmoserschloss, just above town. This is a fairy-tale castle dating back to the days when silver and gold mining flourished in the region; visitors should ask to see the private chapel upstairs.

# OTHER ACTIVITIES

Swimming in thermally heated pools is the main sporting activity apart from skiing, but other traditional pursuits—curling, skating, bowling, tobogganing and walking on prepared trails—are all readily available. The Gastein valley has several cross-country *Loipen* outside the villages, as well as a long one along the river between Bad Hofgastein and Badgastein.

Lying as it does on the railway route between Salzburg and Villach, Bad Hofgastein offers the opportunity to visit either of these cities. Nearer at hand, Bad Hofgastein is the site of what is proudly claimed the largest and most beautiful example of Gothic architecture in the region, the Liebfrauenkirche, built in the 9th century and restored in the 16th. The 18th-century Chapel of St. Anne overlooks the resort from the east and can also be visited.

# BAD KLEINKIRCHHEIM

Access: *Nearest airport:* Klagenfurt (1½ hrs.); Salzburg (2 hrs.).
*By road:* A10 motorway, exit Millstätter See. *By rail:* to Spittal, then by bus.

Tourist Office: A-9546 Bad Kleinkirchheim. Tel. (04240) 82 12

| | |
|---|---|
| Altitude: 1100 m. *Top:* 2055 m. | Ski areas: Kaiserburg, Nockalm, Strohsack |
| Language: German | |
| Beds: 6,000 | Ski schools: Schischule im Grossraum Bad Kleinkirchheim, Schischule St. Oswald |
| Population: 1,800 | |
| Health: Doctors in resort. *Hospital:* Villach (35 km.) | Linked resorts: None |
| Runs: 80 km. | Season: End November to beginning April |
| Lifts: 26 | Kindergarten: *Non-ski:* from 3 years. *With ski:* from 3 years. |

Prices: *Lift pass:* 6 days 1,155–1,285 S (reduction for children). *Ski school:* Group 900 S for 5 days; private 320 S per hour.

# RATINGS

| Skiing Conditions | Snow Conditions | For Beginners | For Intermediates | For Advanced Skiers | For Children | Après-Ski | Other Sports | Value for Money |
|---|---|---|---|---|---|---|---|---|
| 7 | 7 | 5 | 7 | 5 | 6 | 7 | 6 | 7 |

# THE RESORT

Tongue-twisting to Anglo-Saxons, Bad Kleinkirchheim, or BKK as it is more comfortably known, has based much of its publicity on being the place where the incomparable champion Franz Klammer learned to ski. The great man's home is at Mooswald, and he practised his derring-do on the slopes of this old Carinthian spa town and its neighbour, St. Oswald, in Austria's sunny south-east.

Thermal springs were harnessed for bathing by the Romans,

and several inns are a testament to Bad Kleinkirchheim's days as a staging post on the north side of the Julian Alps. Many of the local people have the high-cheekboned good looks of their Yugoslavian neighbours. The Italian border is also close by.

St. Oswald is a tiny hamlet up the valley, and most of the accommodation is at nearby Kirchleiten and Unterkirchleiten, where the farmers' village—an old-style, newly constructed cluster of sturdy two-storey apartment buildings—is ranged around a central complex of bars, restaurant, bowling hall and nightclub.

# THE SKIING

There is, inevitably, a FIS downhill course named after Franz Klammer and another one, from the Strohsack (1910 m.), used for occasional World Cup races. But most of the skiing is straight-forward, fast and undemanding—perfect for intermediates but not ideal for novices, who will find the lift system too dispersed for comfort.

A few short, steep mogul fields served by the Hirschsprunglift test experts, who should go off piste with a guide for real adventure. The quad chair to the west of town has eased bottlenecks around the main lifts in the mornings. The red run is an intermediate's delight, facilitating long swooping turns right down to the bottom.

The skiing area above St. Oswald has only one, very short, black run. The rest of the marked trails are like those in Bad Kleinkirchheim, and there is a variety of lovely off-piste routes through the trees.

A well-intentioned bus service connects the various access points, but unless you have your own car, be prepared for some walking.

The bars and restaurants on the mountainside are friendly, and the clientele less self-conscious than in some of the Alps' best-known places. BKK and St. Oswald are perfect for moderate-ly good skiers who enjoy relaxed on-piste skiing, usually under a sunny sky.

# APRÈS-SKI

The Carinthians are a carefree, merry people and nightlife reflects their approach to life. Bars and cafés are mostly relaxed and informal, as are the discos.

The valley has for centuries been a thoroughfare for European travellers, meaning that the hotel business is long established. The Trattlerhof, with swimming pool, Jacuzzi, sauna and its own riding stables, is one of the best. It is both stylish and traditional, with two restaurants, one a large dining room, the other a snug *Stube* for traditional Carinthian dishes, and the owners organize skiing groups for guests. It has its own pub-style bar close by, with a curling rink right outside.

# OTHER ACTIVITIES

Curling, accompanied by flagons of piping hot *Glühwein*, is great fun after indulging yourself at one of the two thermally heated swimming pools, where all sorts of health treatments are available. A dozen hotels have their own pool, and there is an indoor tennis centre, bowling, squash and 20 km. of prepared cross-country tracks (with access to a further 40 km. in neighbouring regions). Bad Kleinkirchheim is fast developing a reputation as a golfing centre; golf and motor racing are the new-found passions of Herr Klammer.

From BKK, you can make an excursion to the university town of Klagenfurt.

# BRAND

Access: *Nearest airport:* Zurich (2½ hrs.). *By road:* A14 motorway, exit Feldkirch or Bludenz. *By rail:* to Bludenz, then by bus.
Tourist Office: A-6708 Brand. Tel. (05559) 555

Altitude: 1050 m. *Top:* 1920 m.

Language: German

Beds: 2,200

Population: 650

Health: Doctor and hospital in Bludenz (11 km.).

Runs: 40 km.

Lifts: 13

Ski areas: Palüd, Niggenkopf, Melkboden

Ski schools: Schischule Brand

Linked resorts: None (link to Bürserberg for 1989)

Season: Mid-December to beginning of April

Kindergarten: *Non-ski*: 1–5 years. *With ski:* from 4 years.

Prices: *Lift pass:* 6 days 1,195 S (children 720 S). *Ski school:* Group 990 S for 5 days; private 400 S per hour.

# RATINGS

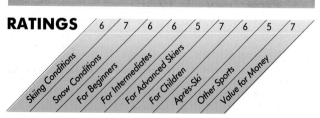

| Skiing Conditions | Snow Conditions | For Beginners | For Intermediates | For Advanced Skiers | For Children | Après-Ski | Other Sports | Value for Money |
|---|---|---|---|---|---|---|---|---|
| 6 | 7 | 6 | 6 | 5 | 7 | 6 | 5 | 7 |

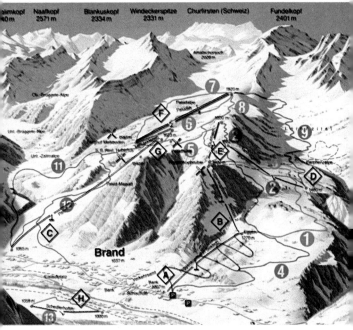

# THE RESORT

Since the first settlers journeyed from the Swiss Valais, arriving in the Brandnertal in 1347, Brand has developed into a thriving and sophisticated year-round centre for tourism, in sharp contrast to the harsh environment experienced by the villagers' ancestors who were impoverished cattle herdsmen, battling to survive in an inhospitable valley.

But today hospitality is the hallmark of this Vorarlberg village in the Rätikon Alps. It is perennially popular with British guests, some of whom have been visiting for over 40 years, and tends to attract the discerning self-drive market.

## THE SKIING

Painstaking piste maintenance is a feature on the Palüd and Niggenkopf slopes, which are fed by chair lifts from both ends of town. Each has a restaurant at the top, from where a network of T-bars rises above the tree line, some of them serving secluded off-piste routes back to the valley and others a mixture of blue and red trails, mostly cut wide, with imposing views all round. The summit is at 1920 m., from where the red-graded Lorenzital trail leads back to the base of Tannlegerlift—a lovely quiet run which is closed at the first indication of avalanche danger.

Bürserberg is a separate area just outside Bludenz. It is planned to open a link system with Brand for the 1989 season. Bürserberg is included on the same lift pass and is worth a couple of days examination—the terrain is similar to that of Brand and the lift pass allows free use of the bus between the villages.

Although there isn't a ski school race as such, the weekly guest race takes place under lights on the slopes nearest the village, and there is a children's category.

## APRÈS-SKI

With a pub named the Britannia in town, don't expect the worst! It is a jolly, verging on rowdy, place at times, but is a singular ingredient in Brand's mix of restaurants specializing in Swiss-influenced *nouvelle cuisine,* middle of the road entertainment at the Valbona Bar and the big disco at the Scesa Taverna. There is talk of the tea dances at the Hotel Scesaplana being revived to fill the gap between skiing and a sauna before dinner.

## OTHER ACTIVITIES

The Hotel Scesaplana has indoor tennis courts and, with more due for opening in the Lagant complex, there will be a thoroughly viable alternative to skiing when the weather closes in. Bowling takes place on two lanes in the Sarotla, while the Lagant and Zaluanda both have pools open to non-residents. Horse riding and sleigh-rides are available, while the more adventurous can join the hang-gliding school. The 3½-km. floodlit toboggan run is reached by taking the double chair lift to the top of the

Niggenkopf run. Brand is a good cross-country skiing area with 17 km. of trails close by and a further 17 km. around Bürserberg.

Bludenz, a textile town also known for its chocolate-making, is at the junction of five valleys. Its centre is traffic-free and the weekly food market is an interesting diversion, particularly if you are self-catering. Both Zurich and Innsbruck are two hours away by rail, and Vaduz, capital of Liechtenstein, can be reached by train and bus.

# ELLMAU

Access: *Nearest airport:* Munich (2½ hrs.). *By road:* A12 motorway, exit Wörgl-Ost. *By rail:* to Kufstein, then by bus.
Tourist Office: A-6352 Ellmau. Tel. (05358) 23 01

| | |
|---|---|
| Altitude: 820 m. *Top:* 1829 m. | Lifts: 12 (86 in Wilder Kaiser-Brixental) |
| Language: German | Ski areas: Astberg, Hartkaiser |
| Beds: 4,900 | Ski schools: Tiroler Schischule Ellmau |
| Population: 1,900 | |
| Health: Doctors and dentist in resort. *Hospital:* St. Johann (10 km.) | Linked resorts: Going, Scheffau, Söll, Brixen, Hopfgarten, Itter |
| Runs: 35 km. (200 km. in Wilder Kaiser-Brixental) | Season: December to April |
| | Kindergarten: *Non-ski:* none. *With ski:* from 4 years. |

Prices: *Lift pass:* 6 days 1,000 S (children 580 S). *Ski school:* Group 340 S per day; private 320 S per hour.

# RATINGS

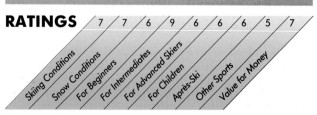

| Skiing Conditions | Snow Conditions | For Beginners | For Intermediates | For Advanced Skiers | For Children | Après-Ski | Other Sports | Value for Money |
|---|---|---|---|---|---|---|---|---|
| 7 | 7 | 6 | 9 | 6 | 6 | 6 | 5 | 7 |

*For map, see p. 202.*

# THE RESORT

Ellmau is a small and friendly village, less well known but prettier than its neighbour, Söll. Its main problem is that, whilst it would be pleasant to wander its streets at leisure, this is impossible due to a steady wave of motor vehicles looking for somewhere to park; the self-drive Dutch and, particularly, German market has homed-in on Ellmau. At night, with the tiny chapel immediately above the village illuminated, it is one of the Tyrol's most seductive villages.

# THE SKIING

The resort has access to the Skigrossraum Wilder Kaiser-Brixental area shared with Going, Scheffau, Söll, Itter, Hopfgarten and Brixen. Westendorf, reached via Brixen or Hopfgarten by free bus, is also included on the pass.

For all but the very best skiers there are limitless opportunities to bash around the Grossraum, taking the 200-km. circuit at full tilt, relishing in the several testing runs along the way. The funicular railway runs from outside the village (Ellmau doesn't provide the easiest access for skiing in the Alps) to Hartkaiser (1555 m.), from where skiers disperse to adjacent Scheffau or over the Eiberg (1673 m.) or Zinsberg (1674 m.) to Brixen.

To reach Söll, Itter and Hopfgarten, ski around the Grossraum's highest point, the Hohe Salve (1829 m.), but be sure to catch the last connecting lift home as, although each resort has its own free ski-bus service, none link the villages. To be stranded at Brixen at the end of the day entails a complicated journey by post bus or an expensive taxi ride. Ellmau's skiing connects to, but not back from, Going—another pretty village. Beginners have their own nursery apron and lifts right outside the village centre. Slopes are north-east facing so that snow lasts longer than in, say, Brixen—on the south-facing side of the Grossraum.

# APRÈS-SKI

Sleigh-rides, Tyrolean evenings, bars and discos (Ellmauer Tenne and Rossstall are very popular with Britons) constitute the region's standard mix of après-ski activities.

57

# OTHER ACTIVITIES

There is a 10-km. cross-country trail in the immediate vicinity and plenty more further along the Leukental, as well as 55 km. of prepared walks. Ellmau's 4½-km. illuminated toboggan course is considered one of the best, and safest, in the region, and skating is available on a natural rink which is only open when weather conditions permit. Curling takes place on both natural and artificial surfaces. Three hotels have bowling; one has a swimming pool open to the public and two more have pools for their guests.

Excursions to Innsbruck and Salzburg are available, while the post bus runs to Kitzbühel, providing the chance to indulge in some expensive shopping, as well as sampling one of Europe's most famous skiing areas.

# FIEBERBRUNN

⛷ ⛷ ⛷

Access: *Nearest airport:* Munich (2½ hrs.). *By road:* A12 motorway, exit Kufstein-Süd. *By rail:* railway station in Fieberbrunn.
Tourist Office: A-6391 Fieberbrunn. Tel. (05354) 63 05

Altitude: 800 m. *Top:* 1800 m.

Language: German

Beds: 3,900

Population: 3,900

Health: Doctors in resort.
*Hospital:* St. Johann (10 km.)

Runs: 60 km.

Lifts: 14

Ski areas: Lärchfilzkogel, Streuböden, Hochkogel

Ski schools: Schischule Fieberbrunn im Tirol

Linked resorts: None

Season: Beginning December to end April

Kindergarten: *Non-ski:* from 4 years. *With ski:* from 4 years.

Prices: *Lift pass:* 6 days 900–995 S (children 590–640 S). *Ski school:* Group 950 S for 6 days; private 320 S per hour.

## RATINGS

| Skiing Conditions | Snow Conditions | For Beginners | For Intermediates | For Advanced Skiers | For Children | Après-Ski | Other Sports | Value for Money |
|---|---|---|---|---|---|---|---|---|
| 5 | 8 | 7 | 6 | 5 | 6 | 6 | 5 | 7 |

# THE RESORT

This sprawling village, strung out along the Pillerstal with the Pillersache river running alongside, prides itself on being the eastern Tyrol's *Schneewinkl* (snow pocket). Climatic peculiarities provide Fieberbrunn with surprisingly heavy snowfalls—heavier than neighbours St. Johann in Tirol and Kitzbühel—and, being entirely north-facing, the slopes retain their snow cover well into April.

Originally named Pramau, the village takes its name (literally "Fever Well") from the miraculous recovery from illness, in 1354, of Empress Margarete of Tirol and Bavaria who, as a last resort to regain health, took the local waters. The church is especially pretty but, being dispersed, the settlement as a whole lacks the seductive charm of some of its Tyrolean neighbours.

A guest card, included in the price of hotel accommodation, gives discounts on lift passes, insurance, swimming pool, sauna, solarium and ice skating.

Though limited in size for experts, Fieberbrunn is well worth a visit after a heavy snowfall if staying within driving (or short railway journey) distance because the powder skiing is excellent. Otherwise, it is a good place in which to learn and ideal for improving intermediates.

# THE SKIING

There are nursery slopes just to the west of the village centre, and from the Berghaus area—which is the meeting point of three arriving (and one departing) lifts— a long well-pisted blue slope runs back to town with a few detours en route. Most of the remainder of the area is graded red, with the top section of the run down from the Lärchfilzkogel apt to give timid skiers a fright.

The only black run is at Reckmoos—steep and narrow in parts so that it quickly becomes rutted with moguls—but there is plenty of off-piste work to be found, and the ski school specializes in teaching powder technique.

On Sundays there are all-comers' races under the WiSBI handicap scheme providing the opportunity of testing one's aptitude against that of an Austrian champion.

# APRÈS-SKI

Tyrolean evenings (with audience participation encouraged), medieval banquets at the Schloss Einkehr (featuring an eight-course dinner, magic and penalties for failing to observe imbecilic rules), plus fondue suppers preceding the ski school presentation-cum-dance are all popular. Daytime or evening sleigh-rides to Eiserne Hand provide a scenic diversion.

Immediately after skiing there is dancing in a couple of hotels near the base of the lift system and, later on, several discos. The atmosphere is, however, low-key.

# OTHER ACTIVITIES

Bowling evenings at St. Ulrich are good fun. The toboggan run at Gasteig, near St. Johann, is partially floodlit, and the swimming pool has the additional facilities of sauna, solarium, restaurant and bars. Cross-country skiing is good, with four *Loipen* in the immediate vicinity and several more at St. Ulrich, St. Jacob and Hochfilzen (reached by free ski bus). A pleasing variety of cleared paths for walking completes Fieberbrunn's reasonable claim to providing good winter holidays for all generations and aspirations.

The usual excursions for the region—Munich, Kufstein, Berchtesgaden and Salzburg, Innsbruck and Vipiteno—are augmented by visits to Aurach's wildlife park and the *Tiere mit Herz* "Animals with a Heart" cuddly toy factory at the western end of Fieberbrunn.

63

# FILZMOOS

Access: *Nearest airport:* Salzburg (1½ hrs.). *By road:* A10 motorway, exit Eben. *By rail:* to Eben, then by bus.

Tourist Office: A-5532 Filzmoos. Tel. (06453) 235

Altitude: 1057 m. *Top:* 2700 m.

Language: German

Beds: 3,500

Population: 1,100

Health: Doctor in resort. *Hospital:* Schwarzach (40 km.)

Runs: 35 km.

Lifts: 14

Ski areas: Grossberg, Mooslehen, Rossbrand, Rettenstein

Ski schools: Schischule Filzmoos, Schischule Neuberg

Linked resorts: Neuberg

Season: December to April

Kindergarten: *Non-ski:* from 3 years. *With ski:* from 4 years.

Prices: *Lift pass:* 6 days 1,110 S (children 740 S). *Ski school:* Group 950 S for 6 days; private 380 S per hour.

# RATINGS

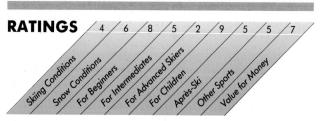

| Skiing Conditions | Snow Conditions | For Beginners | For Intermediates | For Advanced Skiers | For Children | Après-Ski | Other Sports | Value for Money |
|---|---|---|---|---|---|---|---|---|
| 4 | 6 | 8 | 5 | 2 | 9 | 5 | 5 | 7 |

# THE RESORT

The Bischofsmütze mountain, its twin towers looking just like a bishop's mitre, gazes down on this picturesque little village. Perfect for families, it has a children's ski school, and if there are non-skiers in the party, they will enjoy the lovely paths through the woods, specially cleared for walking.

There is a long tradition of tourism here, the village having been popular with well-to-do Viennese before World War I. Filzmoos is close to the border with predominantly Protestant Styria. As recently as the early part of this century, the church bells tolled in misery, and warning, if a local girl crossed the border to marry a Ramsau lad. There is nothing deceptive about the village's prettiness—the local people are friendly, the skiing undaunting and the nightlife cosy.

The favourite hotel for British guests, and a sprinkling of Dutch and Germans, is the Alpenkrone, run by the brother of actress Susan Hampshire. John and his Austrian wife, Rosi, have a particularly good understanding of the needs of British families

Bischofsmütze 2454 m

Hofpürglhütte 1705 m

Sulzenalm 1534 m

Hofalm 1268 m

Aualm 1366 m

1300 m

1361 m

SKISCHAUKEL FILZM

Schwaigalmlift
1698 m lang

Loipe Neuberg

1119 m

Mooslehen-Doppelsessel
1174 m lang

Geierberglift
714 m lang

NEUBERG
1030 m

Eben-Salzburg

Torstein 2948 m
Mitterspitz 2926 m
Hoher Dachstein 3000 m
Hunerkogel 2700 m

Rötelstein 2247 m

826 m

Dachstein Gletscherbahn

Türlwandhütte 1700 m

1540 m

Bachlaim 1495 m

FIS-Strecke

HACHAU 1160 m

Loipe Hachau

Rettensteinlift 2100 m lang

Maosalm 1330 m

ERG

FIS-Strecke

Großberg Sessellift 1100 m lang

FILZMOOS 1057 m

Roßbrandlift 700 m lang

Verbindungslift 592 m lang

Loipe Filzmoos

HANS DANKL·LOFER

and provide a games room for children, so that parents' more serious discussions in the comfortable bar are uninterrupted. The hotel is perched above the village and offers a special bus service for its guests.

# THE SKIING

The three separate mountains, Rettenstein, Rossbrand and Grossberg (the last connecting with Neuberg, a little ski station on the road to Eben), each has limited skiing but not without challenge. Filzmoos produced the great Gitte Totschnig, ladies' downhill champion of the mid-seventies. Now, married to another Austrian Olympic star, Walter Habersatter, she runs the Hotel Olympia next to the nursery slopes—an ideal rendezvous for parents meeting children whose classes finish right outside.

It is generally agreed that the proximity of the Dachstein glacier ensures good snow conditions not enjoyed by other higher centres at the beginning and end of the season, and with slopes facing all round the compass, following the sun around is easy. The children's ski school—teeny tots learning their skills amidst a fantasia of Disney characters—makes Filzmoos a great family favourite. Good skiers shouldn't be put off—individual tuition, making use of the electronically timed, coin-operated slalom course, is attentive and ebullient.

Filzmoos is one of the score or so of resorts in Salzburgerland and Styria covered by the Top-Tauern-Skischeck. Use of a car makes visits to each of the resorts covered by this pass a good day's excursion, but many skiers stay in Filzmoos for its comfortable charm, gorgeous views and tree-lined slopes.

# APRÈS-SKI

Several hotels with live music manage to produce a carefree evening—lively but without the freneticism of some of Austria's better-known centres. That is not to say that Filzmoos is staid, just that it is a village that attracts a clientele which can enjoy a lusty evening without needing a riot.

The Friday afternoon prize-giving ceremony gives children their own après-ski. They all win prizes, and their instructors lead them in enthusiastic dancing.

# OTHER ACTIVITIES

Limited cross-country skiing and walking in the foothills are supplemented by swimming at the sports centre, and there is curling, tobogganing, and an indoor shooting range with weekly competitions.

As well as enjoying the region's natural beauty, you can do a day's excursion to Salzburg.

# FÜGEN

Access: *Nearest airport:* Innsbruck (½ hr.); Munich (1½ hrs.). *By road:* A12 motorway, exit Wiesing/Zillertal. *By rail:* to Jenbach, then by bus or Zillertalbahn.

Tourist Office: A-6263 Fügen. Tel. (05288) 22 62

| | |
|---|---|
| Altitude: 545 m. *Top:* 2050 m. | Ski areas: Spieljoch, Hochfügen (13 km. away, linked by bus) |
| Language: German | |
| Beds: 4,700 | Ski schools: Schischule Fügen/ Hochfügen |
| Population: 3,700 | Linked resorts: None |
| Health: Doctors in resort. *Hospital:* Schwaz (20 km.) | Season: December to end April |
| Runs: 35 km. | Kindergarten: *Non-ski:* none. *With ski:* from 4 years. |
| Lifts: 16 | |

Prices: *Lift pass:* 6 days 950–1,160 S (children 700 S). *Ski school:* Group 950 S for 6 days; private 320 S per hour.

# RATINGS

| Skiing Conditions | Snow Conditions | For Beginners | For Intermediates | For Advanced Skiers | For Children | Après-Ski | Other Sports | Value for Money |
|---|---|---|---|---|---|---|---|---|
| 5 | 5 | 8 | 6 | 3 | 5 | 5 | 4 | 7 |

# THE RESORT

The rambling hillside village of Fügen is the first of several resorts in the Ziller Valley which have become firm favourites among British tour operators and especially popular with families, due to their accessibility and relatively easy skiing. Its Zillertal neighbours, Zell am Ziller and Mayrhofen, are better known and, along with Fügen, are included on the same regional lift pass as Finkenberg, Lanersbach and Hintertux in the Tuxertal, the valley which continues south from Mayrhofen.

# THE SKIING

With its nursery slopes close to most of the major hotels, Fügen is perfect for beginners, who also have some easy skiing around the top station (2087 m.), reached by a two-stage gondola. Although Fügen fails to satisfy the needs of experts (unless they head off through the woods), it is ideal for mixed-ability groups who don't mind hopping onto the local buses and trains (included in the price of a week's lift pass) to explore the rest of the Zillertal and Tuxertal resorts.

Novices have their own terrain, and intermediates who tire of piste-bashing endlessly on the sweeping red run from the summit to middle-station can easily explore the separate skiing area of Hochfügen and take advantage of the efficiently run road and rail systems to Zell am Ziller and Mayrhofen, the latter connecting with Finkenberg.

Should conditions be poor, the glacier at Hintertux guarantees skiing, but be warned: it can be bitterly cold in winter.

There is an all-comers' race each week and everyone qualifies for a gold, silver or bronze award.

# APRÈS-SKI

The Elisabeth, Spieljoch and Kohlerhof are good places to let your hair down at the end of the day—instructors and classes merrily review the day's achievements as soon as the lifts close. Befitting a resort attracting a large number of novices, the highlight of the week is the Ski School Ball when medals and certificates are dispensed, along with great quantities of beer and schnapps.

There are four nightclubs, including the Rockpalast, featuring, as the name suggests, hard rock music, which attracts dancers from all over the valley.

Should a night of writhing to the latest sounds not be your chosen form of entertainment, there are several cosy bars, plus

live music at the Palette, a more intimate place for dancing and chatting. Tour operators organize special Tyrolean evenings complete with wood-chopping contests and drinking games. A more tranquil time can be spent admiring the scenery from a horse-drawn sleigh.

# OTHER ACTIVITIES

The usual Austrian alternatives such as swimming, curling, walking, skating and tobogganing are available, plus crossbow shooting, and there are 40 km. of cross-country *Loipen*.

Innsbruck can be reached by either *Autobahn* or rail (change at Jenbach). The Zillertalbahn a narrow-guage railway, is worth a journey in its own right, trundling along beside the river and terminating at Mayrhofen. In summer a steam locomotive is used, but a more prosaic diesel has to suffice in the winter.

# GALTÜR

Access: *Nearest airport:* Zurich (4 hrs.); Munich (4 hrs.). *By road:* A14 motorway to Bludenz. *By rail:* to Landeck, then by bus.

Tourist Office: A-6563 Galtür/Tyrol. Tel. (05443) 204

Altitude: 1584 m. *Top:* 2300 m.

Language: German

Beds: 3,050

Population: 700

Health: Doctor in resort. *Hospital:* Zams (42 km.)

Runs: 40 km.

Lifts: 11

Ski areas: Birkhahnkopf, Innere Kopsalpe, Alpkogel

Ski schools: Schischule Silvretta-Galtür

Linked resorts: None

Season: Beginning December to beginning April

Kindergarten: *Non-ski:* from 3 years. *With ski:* from 3 years.

Prices: *Lift pass:* 6 days Galtür 960–1,100 S (children 700 S), Silvretta Skipass 1,300–1,540 S (children 900 S). *Ski school:* Group 920 S for 6 days; private 800 S for half-day.

# RATINGS

| Skiing Conditions | Snow Conditions | For Beginners | For Intermediates | For Advanced Skiers | For Children | Après-Ski | Other Sports | Value for Money |
|---|---|---|---|---|---|---|---|---|
| 5 | 7 | 6 | 7 | 6 | 6 | 7 | 6 | 8 |

# THE RESORT

At the far end of the Paznaun valley, beyond Ischgl and close to the Tyrol's border with Vorarlberg, Galtür is an ancient, tiny settlement with most of its skiing above the tree line. Perfect for a no-frills but sophisticated winter holiday, it boasts a few good-

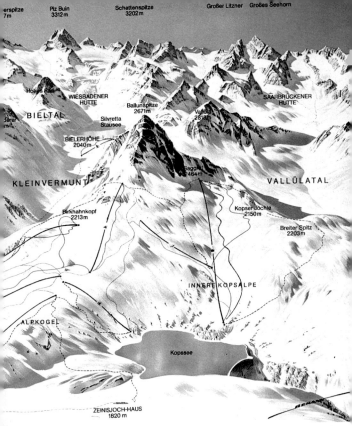

standard hotels, several friendly pensions, a couple of discos and an extraordinarily good sports centre for such a small village. Galtür's reputation as a touring base is long established, and it was Ernest Hemingway's favourite winter retreat for writing and his choice for skiing and walking.

The local dialect is tinged with remnants of the old Romansh language which was originally spoken in this corner of Austria on the border with Switzerland. The beautiful church of St. Maria has had to be rebuilt on several occasions over the centuries as a result of wars with invaders from over the border in the Engadine—the parish priest delights in telling visitors that the local lads always had their revenge by trekking over the border to sack Swiss churches! The resort being small means you can make friends quickly, and it is usual to see the locals working at two, or even three, different locations during the day and evening.

Galtür's remoteness has led to the development of several indigenous culinary specialities, notably the *Paznauner Käsknödelsuppe* (cheese, potato and onion soup) and the valley's own firewater, an Enzian schnapps, tastier and smoother than the mass-produced commercial version.

# THE SKIING

This ranges from an excellent children's ski school to high-alpine touring or heli-skiing. The latter is particularly popular, as the community owns the surrounding mountains, making them impervious to the environmental lobby which has been successful in blocking helicopter landings in other remote parts of Austria; expensive, and subject to disruption by the weather, heli-skiing is truly the ultimate thrill for aficionados. The long history of ski guiding in the Silvretta mountains attracts an international clientele looking for a lot more than piste skiing and chair lifts.

Galtür's on-piste skiing is limited but well maintained with scope for everyone, and the installation of the new four-seater chair lift for the 1988/89 season will surely alleviate the occasional early-morning queues. Several of the lifts serve off-piste runs, notably from the Breitspitz chair lift which offers the opportunity to ski into the Vorarlberg. As the majority of Galtür's visitors drive there, the five-minute journey to and from the village (1584 m.) to Wirl (1635 m.) is a minor hardship and there is a regular, free, bus service.

In a region of abundant snowfalls, good skiing is virtually guaranteed, unless both roads and lifts have to close because there is too much snow. Guests can opt to buy the local pass or a Silvretta ticket which covers all lifts in the valley including those of

Ischgl (20 minutes away by car, a few more by bus) with connections over the Swiss border to Samnaun. So, with only a little enterprise, it is quite feasible to sample some of the best skiing in Austria and to have a charming village as your base.

## APRÈS-SKI

The absence of Tyrolean evenings and sleigh-rides is a telling testament to Galtür's non-commercial atmosphere, but the resort does not lack opportunities for a thoroughly energetic time at night, starting with the traditional daily tea dance at the Wirlerhof (there is also live music in the evening). At around the same time, cafés in the village start to fill and the disco in the Post does a good trade. The major hotels all have live entertainment at least once a week—zithers, one-man bands and groups specializing in Tyrolean and modern international dance music.

## OTHER ACTIVITIES

The sport centre has two tennis courts, a squash court, a 25-m. swimming pool (free admission with local ski pass), three bowling lanes, as well as a café and restaurant. Tobogganing takes place on a floodlit course, and the local sport is manoeuvring down the mountain on bow-shaped skis. The *Langlauf* season is long and the scenery spectacular. There are 45 km. of cross-country trails in the immediate vicinity, and a 10-km. route to Ischgl where there is another large *Loipe*. Weather permitting, skating and curling are available. Hang-gliding and para-ski are among the more adventurous alternative pursuits on offer.

# HINTERTUX/ LANERSBACH

Access: *Nearest airport:* Munich (2 hrs.); Innsbruck (1½ hrs.). *By road:* A12 motorway, exit Wiesing/Zillertal. *By rail:* to Mayrhofen, then by bus.

Tourist Office: A-6293 Lanersbach. Tel. (05287) 606

Altitude: 1300 m. (Lanersbach) *Top:* 3268 m.

Language: German

Beds: 4,200 in Tuxertal

Population: 1,730 in Tuxertal

Health: Doctor in resort. *Hospital:* Schwaz (50 km.)

Runs: 122 km. in Tuxertal

Lifts: 32 in Tuxertal

Ski areas: Tuxer Gletscher, Scheidegg, Lämmerbichl, Eggalm, Sommerbergalm

Ski schools: Schischule Lanersbach, Schischule Hintertux

Linked resorts: None

Season: End November to mid-May; year-round skiing on glacier

Kindergarten: *Non-ski:* from 2 years. *With ski:* from 4 years.

Prices: *Lift pass:* 6 days 950–1,160 S (children 700 S). *Ski school:* Group 880–950 S for 6 days; private 340 S per hour.

## RATINGS

| Skiing Conditions | Snow Conditions | For Beginners | For Intermediates | For Advanced Skiers | For Children | Après-Ski | Other Sports | Value for Money |
|---|---|---|---|---|---|---|---|---|
| 6 | 9 | 3 | 6 | 5 | 4 | 5 | 5 | 5 |

# THE RESORTS

Beyond the hectic hurly-burly of the Ziller Valley and its popular ski centres, the Tuxertal snakes its way up to the foothills beneath the Hintertux glacier, one of Austria's major year-round skiing areas. Hintertux and Lanersbach—just 7 km. back down the valley—are both included on the Zillertal regional lift pass but, being at the far end of the system, neither is ideally situated for exploring neighbouring skiing areas or venturing further afield.

The biggest advantage in visiting Hintertux is that, with much of its skiing on the glacier, good snow conditions are guaranteed. This is offset by occasional extreme cold in December and January. Lanersbach will, one day, be linked with Finkenberg and thence Mayrhofen. Before that happens, take advantage of the fact that most visitors to Mayrhofen fail to make full use of the Zillertal lift pass and those that do bypass Lanersbach's skiing for the better-known slopes of Hintertux.

In summer, this is a valley of outstanding beauty—cow bells tinkle on mountain pastures, wooden-galleried farmhouses drip with geraniums, and icy rivulets work their way from the glacier through sparkling forests to the valley—and skiers practise their craft on sun-kissed slopes.

# THE SKIING

Lanersbach is the largest of the Tuxertal villages but has the smallest skiing system, rising from 1300 m. to the Eggalm summit (2500 m.), below which the restaurant has fabulous views of the Zillertal Alps. All of the skiing is easy, either on the wide, open upper area or through trees back to the village.

Hintertux has much more variety and is the pre-season training ground for several World Cup squads. The two-stage gondola has a large car park at its base and rises to the Sommerbergalm which is, as its name indicates, the starting point of the summer skiing area—its restaurant takes on a Riviera-like aspect in July, bikini-clad sunbathers relaxing on the terrace after the snow has become too slushy in the early-afternoon sun.

In winter, the upper glacial slopes can be windswept and bitterly cold but, lower down, you have more protection from the elements by taking trails through the trees.

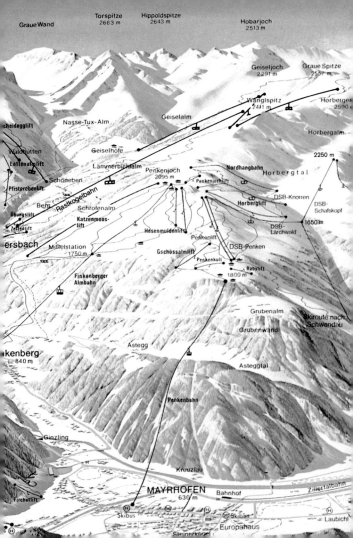

# APRÈS-SKI

For a hectic night out, it is necessary to take a taxi down to Mayrhofen because, although welcoming, both Lanersbach and Hintertux are small with just a handful of cafés and one or two disco-bars. Despite is homely appearance, Hintertux has a few good hotels, notably the Kirchler, which has a friendly *Stuberl* bar, a pool and dancing.

# OTHER ACTIVITIES

Some hotels allow non-residents to use their pools and fitness facilities; otherwise there is a thermal pool. Skibob, tobogganing, bowling and curling are all available, although, as the settlements are spread out along the valley, moving from one activity to another is inconvenient without a car. Cross-country skiers can enjoy 25 km. of tracks; walkers have 20 km. of cleared paths.

# HOCHKÖNIG

Access: *Nearest airport:* Salzburg (1 hr.); Munich (2 hrs.). *By road:* A12 motorway, exit Kufstein. *By rail:* to Bischofshofen, then by bus.

Tourist Office: A-5505 Mühlbach. Tel. (06467) 235
A-5652 Dienten. Tel. (06461) 263

Altitude: 854 m. (Mühlbach), 1071 m. (Dienten) *Top:* 1900 m.

Language: German

Beds: 1,870 in Mühlbach, 1,150 in Dienten

Population: 1,658 in Mühlbach, 816 in Dienten

Health: Doctor in Mühlbach. *Hospital:* Schwarzach (20 km.)

Runs: 150 km.

Lifts: 45

Ski areas: Maria Alm, Hintermoos, Hinterthal, Dienten, Mühlbach

Ski schools: Schischule Plenk-Mühlbach, Schischule Dienten

Linked resorts: None

Season: December to April

Kindergarten: *Non-ski:* from 3 years. *With ski:* from 4 years.

Prices: *Lift pass:* 6 days 840–930 S (children 560–625 S). *Ski school:* Group 950 S for 6 days; private 380 S per hour.

# RATINGS

| Skiing Conditions | Snow Conditions | For Beginners | For Intermediates | For Advanced Skiers | For Children | Après-Ski | Other Sports | Value for Money |
|---|---|---|---|---|---|---|---|---|
| 5 | 5 | 5 | 7 | 5 | 6 | 5 | 5 | 6 |

## THE RESORTS

These Salzburgerland villages of Maria Alm, Hintermoos, Hinterthal, Dienten and Mühlbach take their collective name from the Hochkönig outcrop (2941 m.) which dominates the area, and if none of them rates more than a passing reference in its own right, they combine to provide beginners and intermediates with an excellent ''ski shuttle'' from one end of the network and back again.

It is a pretty area, usually bypassed by keen skiers *en route* to

HOHE TAUERN

Klingspitz

Salzachtal
Lend

WASTLHÖHE 1737 m

X

Bürglalm

E

11

11

DIENTEN
am Hochkönig

Eisschießb.

Z 15

13

Y

F

G

Hochkönigloipe

12

12

Taghaube
2159 m

Alpengasthof
Übergossene Alm
1240 m

Matrash

HOCHK(
2941

bigger centres in the region, and is largely undiscovered by British tour operators. Indeed, one eminent Fleet Street travel editor has studiously kept it a secret from his readers so that his own family skiing holidays take place on uncrowded slopes.

Maria Alm is at the westerly end of the (not-completely-linked) lift system; Mühlbach, to the east, is beyond Bischofshofen. Each of the villages is unspoiled, despite a good deal of construction in the last few years—the regional architectural style has been

Kitzsteinhorn 3203 m

Hundstein 2117 m

8 m

ZellamSee ↓

Langeck

GABÜHEL 1634 m

Aberg

21

J

22

Hintermoos

Gamsbichl
Hütte

K

H

L

L

Maria

24

Filzensattel

● oberschneider

painstakingly preserved. British school-parties account for the largest non-Austrian clientele.

Anyone used to purpose-built, high-rise resorts will find that there is more walking than in one of the big French centres or those in Austria with fully-interlinked skiing areas, but the compensations are the region's prettiness, the friendliness of the local people and the grandeur of the Hochkönig, its peak picked out in a pink hue in the late afternoon sun.

# THE SKIING

Although there are one or two surprises for the unwary, this is a perfect area for novices and improving intermediates. Each village has nursery areas separate from the *Schischaukel* (the runs which connect the villages), so that beginners can practise in peace before graduating to the more demanding trails aloft.

Mühlbach has a couple of lifts right in the village centre, and its main area, just outside town and served by free bus, has some lovely, fast trails over to Dienten. To continue the network, it is necessary to walk across the road and take a chair lift to the Gamsbichl Hütte. From here, you can choose to ski down to Hinterthal and take a bus to Hintermoos, or stop halfway and take the Hochmaisgipfel lift for a choice of unpisted routes to the same destination.

With 150 km. of marked trails, it is a large area, but real experts will find that it is frustrating to have to take skis on and off if they want to hit the slopes all day long. Less experienced skiers should be happy cruising around the trails in their immediate vicinity, with the occasional foray further afield. If you have a car, day trips to Lofer and Leogang, which are included on a special regional pass, give extra variety.

# APRÈS-SKI

Low-key, informal and oozing with *Gemütlichkeit,* the villages have an easy, unpretentious charm, and evenings can be spent happily chatting around an open fire, dancing to bands specializing in regional music and bopping in merry little disco bars.

# OTHER ACTIVITIES

There are cross-country *Loipen* at Maria Alm, Hinterthal and Dienten; Maria Alm has curling, tobogganing, bowling, sleigh-rides and cleared paths for walking; there is tobogganing and curling in Mühlbach.

Bischofshofen is a good shopping centre, and there are excursions to Salzburg. The few tour operators in the area organize a variety of trips, including visits to the thermal baths in the Gastein Valley and the salt mines at Hallein.

# INNSBRUCK

Access: *Nearest airport:* Innsbruck; Munich (2–2½ hrs.). *By road:* A12 motorway. *By rail:* railway station in Innsbruck.

Tourist Office: A-6021 Innsbruck. Tel. (05222) 25 71 5

Altitude: 580 m. *Top:* 2340 m.

Language: German

Beds: 9,500

Population: 120,000

Health: Doctors, dentists and hospital in Innsbruck

Runs: 75 km.

Lifts: 33

Ski areas: Hungerburg-Seegrube, Mutters-Muttereralm, Igls-Patscherkofel, Tulfes-Glungezer, Axamer Lizum

Ski schools: Schischule Innsbruck, Schischule Renato Huemer (Igls), Schischule Erlacher (Patsch), Schischule Otto Peer (Mutters), Schischule Glungezer (Tulfes), Schischule Axamer Lizum

Linked resorts: None

Season: End December to end March

Kindergarten: *Non-ski:* in Igls, from 3 years. *With ski:* in Igls and Gramar/Hoch-Innsbruck, from 4 years; in Axamer Lizum, from 3 years.

Prices: *Lift pass:* 6 days 1,230 S (children 915 S). *Ski school:* Group 330 S per day; private 310 S per hour.

# RATINGS

| Skiing Conditions | Snow Conditions | For Beginners | For Intermediates | For Advanced Skiers | For Children | Après-Ski | Other Sports | Value for Money |
|---|---|---|---|---|---|---|---|---|
| 7 | 5 | 4 | 8 | 6 | 7 | 9 | 7 | 8 |

# THE RESORT

Host to the Winter Olympics in 1964 and 1976, the capital of the Tyrol isn't really a ski resort in its own right, but it is a fascinating place to stay while sampling the five ski resorts included on the city lift pass, none of them more than a half-hour ride on the free buses which disperse skiers to the mountains each morning. The city is perfect for an all-round winter holiday, soaring peaks gazing down on the elegant shopping arcades, museums and galleries, with all sorts of sporting activities close at hand.

The five resorts covered by the Innsbruck lift pass are Hungerburg, Tulfes, Mutters, Igls and Axamer Lizum, the last-named constructed specifically for the 1964 Olympics. Tulfes and Mutters are both tiny Tyrolean hamlets; Axamer Lizum is a lively purpose-built centre with accommodation right by the slopes; and Igls is a lovely village, much favoured by British visitors who enjoy its traditional charms, and it is also the site of the Olympic bobsleigh and luge circuit. En route from the city, you pass the ski-jump arena, its top station perched precariously above a precipice. The view from the top: a chilling panorama of the city cemetery! Hungerburg is no more than a small and steep skiing area with a restaurant perched high above Innsbruck, affording magnificent views.

Innsbruck is especially good for intermediate skiers who want to enjoy the variety of the five areas and all the other sports facilities close by. Of the outlying ski stations, Igls is the best for a traditional Austrian skiing holiday, with all the delights of the city just 15 minutes down the mountain.

# THE SKIING

Hungerburg is closest to Innsbruck, its funicular railway starting from just outside the centre, and has the toughest but most limited skiing. Tulfes and Mutters have long, wide easy trails cut through the conifers, informal and friendly mountain restaurants, and are perfect for a day's fast cruising and for beginners. Igls shared the Alpine events in both Olympics with Axamer Lizum and is on the itinerary of every self-respecting Austrian who wants to emulate the national hero, Franz Klammer, on the Patscherkofel downhill course—his gold-medal run in 1976 remains one of sport's most

thrilling moments. Axamer Lizum is further from Innsbruck and, being the largest, is the best bet at weekends, when the smaller centres tend to be crowded with local families.

Tuition is available at each of the resorts, and the Innsbruck ski school always has a platoon of instructors at the Landestheater square, from where the free buses fan out to the different resorts each morning. They are delighted to act as guides for the day as well as giving tuition.

There is year-round skiing on the Stubai glacier and excellent cross-country plus some downhill skiing at Seefeld, both of them about 40 minutes drive from the city centre.

## APRÈS-SKI

Being a city of 120,000 inhabitants, Innsbruck is inevitably different from most other ski resorts. Immediately after skiing, the bars around Igls and Axamer Lizum, particularly, engender a typical Tyrolean atmosphere. In town, however, there is a more sophisticated environment, not hell-bent on supplying the needs of exuberant skiers.

There are a few international hotels and many old inns—renovated to the highest of modern standards—which have bars, restaurants and nightclubs. The Schwarzer Adler in Kaiser-jägerstrasse is bedecked with hand-painted furniture and houses a famed restaurant in typical old Tyrolean rooms dating back 400 years; the Goldener Adler was founded in 1390 and its several restaurants and bars are redolent of a bygone age. The atmosphere is sedate, charming and timeless as you are waited on by *Dirndl*-clad waitresses and solicitous waiters in breeches.

There are plenty of lively places, too, including discos or the Piano Bar where local musicians play for beer-money and it is usual to strike up conversation with the people at your table. Just to show that Innsbruck isn't completely steeped in the past, there is a branch of McDonald's in Maria-Theresien-Strasse. Innsbruck's smart set congregates in the Café Club Filou, just inside the walls of the Altstadt.

# OTHER ACTIVITIES

Early in the season, it is possible to take a ride on the Olympic bobsleigh course, a nerve-racking shuddering descent, above the village of Igls, and in the spring months there are Austrian League football matches. Innsbruck's hosting of the Olympic Games produced an excellent ice stadium which is open to the public and stages thrilling ice-hockey matches. There is little cross-country skiing in the immediate vicinity of the city but plenty at Seefeld. That being said, it is commonplace to see families out together at weekends on unmarked cross-country routes, enjoying the splendour of their mountains.

Run of the mill activities include swimming, bowling, tennis, squash and horse riding, not to mention hang-gliding.

Innsbruck is the place that visitors to the rest of the Tyrol go to sightsee: its historic buildings, museums and Alpenzoo. In addition, only 15 minutes away, Hall in Tirol is a brooding, medieval town with twisting, cobbled streets.

The Tiroler Landesreisebüro organizes excursions further afield to Ischgl, St. Anton, Hintertux, Kitzbühel and the Pitztal glacier for skiing, as well as trips to the Bavarian castles and Oberammergau, Zurich, the casino at Seefeld and even as far away as Vienna and Venice.

With a car, a journey south over the Brenner Pass to Vipiteno and the Italian Südtirol is an interesting education in the mixture of Austrian and Italian cultures which have coexisted uneasily since the region was ceded to Italy after World War I.

# ISCHGL

Access: *Nearest airport:* Zurich (2 hrs.); Munich (2 hrs.). *By road:* A14 motorway to Bludenz, then via Arlbergtunnel and Landeck. *By rail:* to Landeck, then by bus.

Tourist Office: A-6561 Ischgl. Tel. (05444) 52 66

| | |
|---|---|
| Altitude: 1400 m. *Top:* 2800 m. | Ski areas: Fimbatal, Velilltal, Idalp, Alp Trida, Hölltal, Vesil |
| Language: German | Ski schools: Schischule Ischgl |
| Beds: 6,000 | Linked resorts: Samnaun |
| Population: 1,100 | Season: December to end April |
| Health: Doctor in resort. *Hospital:* Zams (30 km.) | Kindergarten: *Non-ski:* from 4 years. *With ski:* from 4 years. |
| Runs: 150 km. | |
| Lifts: 34 | |

Prices: *Lift pass:* 6 days Ischgl-Samnaun 1,230-1,470 S (children 880 S). *Ski school:* Group 340 S per day; private 700 S for 2 hours.

# RATINGS

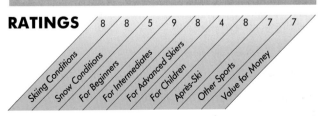

| Skiing Conditions | Snow Conditions | For Beginners | For Intermediates | For Advanced Skiers | For Children | Après-Ski | Other Sports | Value for Money |
|---|---|---|---|---|---|---|---|---|
| 8 | 8 | 5 | 9 | 8 | 4 | 8 | 7 | 7 |

# THE RESORT

Ischgl is the best known of the Paznaun valley resorts and, as well as being available on the same regional pass as Tyrolean neighbours Galtür, Kappl and See, has direct links on skis with Samnaun, a duty-free village over the Swiss border. Ischgl attracts a mostly well-to-do crowd which doesn't mind paying quite high prices for an atmosphere of exclusivity without it being especially glamorous. The surrounding Silvretta range affords astonishing views, seemingly boundless skiing and an outstanding snow record.

Although much of the village is modern, it has charm and an interesting history—originally "Yscla", its first inhabitants trekked over from the Swiss Engadine, and the old Romansh language is reflected in the local Tyrolean patois of today.

A very modern lift system, designed so that little walking is necessary, sometimes fails to cope with German weekend visitors, many of whom stay outside Ischgl and drive in daily. The other problem is that there is occasionally too much snow, avalanche warnings closing the road up from Landeck as well as some of the cross-country trails in the valley. But Ischgl is highly popular with its regular visitors who feel that these are minor inconveniences when the variety of skiing, on and off piste, and a very good selection of hotels, cafés, discos and nightclubs is such that Ischgl ranks as one of Austria's top centres.

The tourist office's "What, When, Where and How in Ischgl" leaflet is among the best of such documents available and itemizes just about every place of entertainment, every type of shop, the regular weekly programme of events, plus full details of every skiing requirement and other sports facilities.

# THE SKIING

Three gondola cableways leave the village from various points, two of them converging on the main Idalp dispersal point which is also the ski-school meeting place, with additional facilities such as restaurants, an ice bar, shops and day nursery. To the north, a network of lifts serve the beginners section, as well as the black runs down from the Pardatsch-Grat (2624 m.) and the longer red trail below Velillscharte (2556 m.).

In the opposite direction, the Hölltal and Vesil areas have a lot of challenging on-piste skiing and excursions through the trees to Bodenalp (1840 m.) or Paznauner Taja where there are several *Gasthöfe*, plus a splendid variety of off-piste options. (In view of the history of avalanches in the region they should only be tried in the company of a guide or, at the very least, with official confirmation of their safety.)

Apart from skiing back to Ischgl, the other options from Idalp are to ski onto the Swiss side, either all the way down to Samnaun (walk or take the bus to the Ravaisch to return) or concentrate on the Alp Trida section where there are more opportunities to sample off-piste skiing and a few red-graded pistes—restaurants on the Swiss side are even more expensive than they are on the Ischgl side.

Ischgl has just about the full gamut of skiing. It is a large area served by 34 lifts, but unless real experts indulge in powder skiing, there are few really testing marked runs. As well as the ski-school races, all-comers' guest races on Thursdays are popular, and the ski kindergarten takes place around Idalp so that parents can meet their offspring for lunch and return home together at the end of the day.

The local lift pass covers Ischgl and Samnaun, whilst the Silvretta ticket allows skiing at Galtür, Kappl and See, none of them more than 20 minutes away by car or bus.

# APRÈS-SKI

For early in the evening there are bars such as Café Christine, Taja and the Club Après for energetic drinking sessions and tea dances. Tyrolean evenings at the rather antiseptic Silvretta Centre are a little short on *Gemütlichkeit,* but sleigh-rides through the woods to Mathon engender a more typical Tyrolean feeling. The Silvretta Centre is, however, a well-run venue for a variety of sporting pursuits and shows German-language films. The three main nightclubs (La Not at the Hotel Post, the Hotel Trofana's Tenne and the Madlein Wunderbar) have live bands, and the friendly Club Après disco keeps younger limbs and spirits happy until the early hours. The weekly ski-school presentation is eagerly awaited by participants.

# OTHER ACTIVITIES

The Silvretta Centre is the place for swimming, sauna, steam room, massage and bowling—the last being a feature of tour operators' programmes, which also include evening cross-country tours and tobogganing down the 6-km. course at Kappl (10 mins). Ischgl's own cross-country amounts to about 10 km.; by either taking the bus or skiing all the way to Galtür, there is a further 45 km.—with tuition available, if required.

Duty-free shopping in Samnaun is a chance to do something out of the ordinary. The old village of Mathon, a bus-ride away, has a charming folk museum.

# KIRCHBERG

Access: *Nearest airport:* Munich (1 hr.). *By road:* A12 motorway, exit Wörgl-Ost. *By rail:* railway station in Kirchberg.

Tourist Office: A-6365 Kirchberg. Tel. (05357) 23 09

| | |
|---|---|
| Altitude: 860 m. *Top:* 2000 m. | Lifts: 16 (60 in Skigrossraum) |
| Language: German | Ski areas: Gaisberg, Ehren-bachhöhe, Pengelstein |
| Beds: 8,000 | |
| Population: 3,900 | Ski schools: Schischule Pepi Schoderböck |
| Health: Doctors and dentist in resort.<br>*Hospital:* Kitzbühel (6 km.). | Linked resorts: Kitzbühel, Jochberg, Pass Thurn, Aschau |
| Runs: 40 km. (160 km. in Ski-grossraum) | Season: December to April |
| | Kindergarten: *Non-ski:* from 3 years. *With ski:* from 4 years. |

Prices: *Lift pass:* 6 days 1,390 S (children 695 S). *Ski school:* Group 950 S for 6 days; private 1,000 S for half-day.

# RATINGS

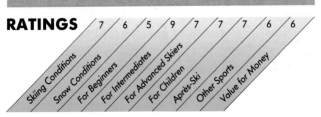

| Skiing Conditions | Snow Conditions | For Beginners | For Intermediates | For Advanced Skiers | For Children | Après-Ski | Other Sports | Value for Money |
|---|---|---|---|---|---|---|---|---|
| 7 | 6 | 5 | 9 | 7 | 7 | 7 | 6 | 6 |

*For map, see p. 111.*

# THE RESORT

On the main Salzburg-Innsbruck railway line between Kitzbühel and Brixen, Kirchberg shares much of Kitzbühel's skiing area but little else. Whereas Kitzbühel attracts an international set, many of whom have little interest in skiing (certainly not on a cold day), Kirchberg has the atmosphere of a happy-go-lucky ski village where fur coats and evening gowns are positively pretentious.

Several lively bars argue against Kirchberg's reputation for being a sleepy suburb of glitzy Kitzbühel, and tour operators offer a full programme of activities, so that Kirchberg quite rightly claims to offer a combination of top-quality skiing and energetic après-ski.

There are a couple of first-grade hotels and plenty more modest places down to the most humble *Gasthof*. Without being especially pretty, Kirchberg is a good place for most skiers, and its only drawbacks are that most of the accommodation is a fair walk from the main lifts (a free bus, however, links hotels and lifts) and that its proximity to Kitzbühel is reflected in quite high prices, which means that beginners or the impecunious might be happier elsewhere.

# THE SKIING

Kirchberg is at the western end of Kitzbühel's Ski Safari which runs to Pass Thurn via Jochberg. It is a 37-km. ski shuttle, fully connected (one way) although a bit of a walk is necessary on arrival in Jochberg.

Kitzbühel is renowned worldwide as a truly great skiing centre, and the main advantage of choosing Kirchberg as a base is that you can avoid the appalling queues for the Hahnenkamm cable car by taking a bus to the Fleckalmbahn gondola or to Kirchberg's own lifts for easier access. The Kitzbüheler Horn, a separate area to the east of Kitzbühel, is also included on the lift pass as are the runs above Aurach from the Stuckkogel. If all this wasn't enough, Kirchberg has its own, separate, slopes on the Gaisberg. Suffice to say, it is a huge network which keeps experts and intermediates thoroughly entertained and, if unfit, exhausted.

## APRÈS-SKI

Fondue nights and sleigh-rides (with accordion music, yodelling and singing at the Achenstüberl) together with the weekly ski school presentation are the main features which, along with bar hopping, discos, a few nightclubs and a couple of Tyrolean bars, make Kirchberg a merry place in the evening. Not as stylish as Kitzbühel, but unpretentious and fun.

## OTHER ACTIVITIES

Bowling evenings at the ancient Gasthof Unterm Rain are popular, with a variety of games and prizes—the latter, invariably, are tots of schnapps. Kirchberg doesn't have its own toboggan run, but tour operators take their guests to Gasteig, near St. Johann, for an evening out. The local skating and curling rinks are sometimes closed after a snowfall, but the weather won't affect swimming in the indoor pool at the sports centre. The cross-country skiing opportunities are legend, with *Loipen* reaching beyond Brixen to Westendorf.

Kitzbühel is but minutes away by bus or train, and the railway connects Kirchberg with other resorts such as Hopfgarten, Westendorf, Brixen, St. Johann in Tirol, Fieberbrunn and Zell am See. There are organized excursions to Berchtesgaden and Salzburg, Innsbruck, and Vipiteno in Italy and to the wildlife park at Aurach.

# KITZBÜHEL

Access: *Nearest airport:* Munich (1 hr.). *By road:* A12 motorway, exit Kufstein-Süd. *By rail:* railway station in Kitzbühel.

Tourist Office: A-6370 Kitzbühel. Tel. (05356) 22 72

| | |
|---|---|
| Altitude: 800 m. *Top:* 2000 m. | Ski areas: Hahnenkamm, Kitzbüheler Horn, Ehrenbachhöhe, Pengelstein |
| Language: German | |
| Beds: 8,000 | Ski schools: Rote Teufel Schischule |
| Population: 8,000 | |
| Health: Doctors and hospital in Kitzbühel | Linked resorts: Pass Thurn, Jochberg, Kirchberg, Aschau |
| Runs: 160 km. in Skigrossraum | Season: December to end April |
| Lifts: 60 in Skigrossraum | Kindergarten: *Non-ski:* 1–5 years. *With ski:* from 3 years. |

Prices: *Lift pass:* 6 days 1,030–1,390 S (children 695 S). *Ski school:* Group 950 S for 6 days; private 1,050 for half-day.

## RATINGS

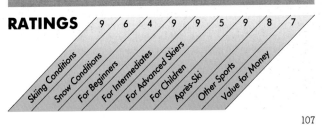

| Skiing Conditions | Snow Conditions | For Beginners | For Intermediates | For Advanced Skiers | For Children | Après-Ski | Other Sports | Value for Money |
|---|---|---|---|---|---|---|---|---|
| 9 | 6 | 4 | 9 | 9 | 5 | 9 | 8 | 7 |

# THE RESORT

In the same way that, say, New York is a great city, Kitzbühel is a great ski resort. But for all the glamour, sophistication, entertainment and sheer wealth that attracts visitors to New York there is an all-too-prevalent seedy side. So, too, in Kitzbühel. To many of the old-money brigade, it remains the *only* place to ski and it is the place to which those with social ambitions aspire. It also attracts a sizeable young yobbo element with more money than drinking capacity.

But if the streets are sometimes noisy, a few of the bars highly boisterous to say the least, and the queues for the Hahnenkamm cable-car tedious, Kitzbühel retains its unique status in the ski world due to several factors. Firstly, there is the great men's World Cup downhill and slalom races every January, rivalled only by Wengen's Lauberhorn descent for the Blue Riband of international racing. The attendant publicity assures Kitzbühel of world-wide recognition as a challenging and exciting skiing area.

The second factor, to the astonishment of many Americans who flock there like pilgrims, is that it is far removed from the picture-book ski *Dorf* depicted on chocolate boxes and calendars. Kitzbühel is a large, thronging town and, instead of sweet little chalets, there is a sturdy medieval centre with large pastel-daubed buildings, the jagged rooftops of which resemble the nearby Wilder Kaiser mountains.

Kitzbühel's long-established hotels, fine clothing shops and excellent restaurants make it a good centre for non-skiers, and with a railway station in town, jaunts to Innsbruck, Salzburg and further afield are easily managed.

Lastly, with only a little initiative, it is possible to find long, uncrowded runs away from the hubbub of poor skiers in danger of slaughtering all around them as they try to emulate their heroes on the Hahnenkamm's Streif downhill course.

Conversation in après-ski bars and mountain restaurants is multi-lingual, Kitzbühel attracting a truly international clientele. If the American visitors who expect a romantic Tyrolean scenario are surprised initially, they quickly become entranced by Kitzbühel's skiing, shopping and sights.

# THE SKIING

For intermediates and experts, Kitzbühel offers skiing un-surpassed in Austria. Even if beginners and children might find somewhere smaller and cheaper more suitable, the great Toni Sailer, whose trio of gold medals at the 1956 Olympics emphasized Kitzbühel's sizeable credentials, runs the children's ski school, and beginners start their tuition on the flat apron at the end of the formidable Streif downhill run on the Hahnenkamm.

With the Hahnenkamm cable car close to the middle of town, access to the slopes would be easier than in most Austrian resorts

were it not for the fact that everyone wants to ride it in the morning. Cognoscenti take the free buses to the Fleckalmbahn gondola station or the Jochberg and Pass Thurn lifts which are usually less crowded. The Fleckalmbahn rises to the Ehrenbachhöhe, the central part of Kitzbühel's lift system which is also reached from Kirchberg, a smaller and less highly pressured village. Jochberg and Pass Thurn (more of which later) are at the far end of Kitzbühel's Ski Safari and are large areas in their own right, interconnecting with each other but only one way with the rest of the system.

Good skiers should certainly try their luck, as well as exerting a

111

considerable amount of skill and nerve, on the Streif... forget that you are an embryonic Franz Klammer and that he and his ilk usually record times around the two-minute mark. The upper parts are frighteningly steep and even if you are an expert skier there is the near certainty that you will have to circumnavigate more nervous, and less talented, brethren strewn about or tentatively side-slipping down parts of the mountain which World Cup racers take in mid-air at 80 mph.

There is good skiing on piste all around the Hahnenkamm area, with a variety of off-piste possibilities as well as some ski routes which, being left unpisted, quickly become mogul infested, notably the Fleckhochalm run.

Beware of taking what appear to be ski routes. The piste map clearly shows controlled pistes and ski routes, and trails are well marked, but there are dozens of occasions during the day when you will see tracks leading down interesting-looking descents. In view of recent avalanche disasters in the Alps, and bearing in mind that even the best of skiers can find themselves in perilous situations on uncharted terrain, heed the local intelligence which dictates that it is thoroughly foolhardy to venture into unknown territory without a qualified guide. With a guide, however, there is some spectacular off-piste skiing all over the Hahnenkamm.

There is still more in the Jochberg and Pass Thurn areas—each would be a sizeable resort in its own right if there was more local accommodation—and the on-piste skiing is generally easy. Again, with a guide, there are scores of off-piste forays through the trees, down steep gullies or on wide walls which require a lot of walking and traversing, but are worth all the effort by providing the ultimate skiing experience of near-vertical drops through pristine powder after a fresh snowfall.

There are two more separate sections of Kitzbühel's portfolio. The Bichlalm is the small area above Aurach (on the road between Kitzbühel and Jochberg) and the Kitzbüheler Horn, disappointing in scope for good skiers but a good choice if you want to avoid the Hahnenkamm's congestion. The slopes being south-facing, conditions are variable. All over the mountains there are restaurants and bars, some rustic, others modern self-service and most of them expensive. If you can avoid the crowds, Kitzbühel offers some of the best skiing in Europe.

# APRÈS-SKI

It's all there—unless you want the steamy log-cabin charm of some of Kitzbühel's more typically Tyrolean counterparts.

Although there are a few bars at the bottom of the slopes, conducive to taking a beer or *Jägertee* immediately after skiing, most people tend either to walk or take a bus to town where they can choose to enjoy an outdoor drink amidst a well-dressed, perfectly coiffeured crowd, join a noisy antipodean booze-up or relax in the hotel bar.

The better hotels have top-quality health and sports facilities, as well as a choice of dining rooms and a nightclub so that there is no need to venture outside. But with Kitzbühel's shops (where you can buy made-to-measure ski pants and custom-made Tyrolean hunting clothing, as well as the very best in ski and leisure wear) and a dazzling array of bars, restaurants and discos from which to choose, it is a shame to miss one of the Alps' great experiences by staying indoors.

Kitzbühel boasts a casino, museums, fashion fairs and a series of concerts. Of the more traditional pursuits, sleigh-rides past the Schwarzsee lake to Schloss Münichau are popular, and medieval banquets, fondue suppers, plus Tyrolean evenings at the ancient Hotel Zur Tenne are featured in tour operators' programmes.

# OTHER ACTIVITIES

The Kitzbühel lift pass allows entry to the Aquarena where there is a health centre, as well as swimming pool, sauna and solarium. Three indoor tennis courts, a squash court, artificial ice rink, indoor curling and a riding school mean that Kitzbühel has plenty to offer in addition to skiing. With 30 km. of cross-country trails close to hand and, in the company of a free guide, a further 200 km. in the region, the town is a true winter sports centre.

It is almost superfluous to mention sightseeing opportunities within reach of Kitzbühel, as for visitors staying in villages all over the eastern Tyrol Kitzbühel is the destination. Being on the mainline railway, however, between Salzburg and Innsbruck, it is within easy reach of both of these exquisite cities.

# LECH

Access: *Nearest airport:* Zurich (2½ hrs.); Munich (1 hr.); Innsbruck (2 hrs.) *By road:* A14 motorway to Bludenz, then via Langen. *By rail:* to Langen, then by bus.

Tourist Office: A-6764 Lech am Arlberg. Tel. (05583) 21 61 0

Altitude: 1450 m. *Top:* 2377 m.

Language: German

Beds: 6,700

Population: 1,270

Health: Doctors and fracture clinic in resort.
*Hospital:* Bludenz (40 km.)

Runs: 110 km. with Zürs (300 km. in Arlberg area)

Lifts: 33 with Zürs (74 in Arlberg area)

Ski areas: Kriegerhorn, Oberlech, Rüfikopf

Ski schools: Schischule Lech, Schischule Oberlech

Linked resorts: Zürs, Zug

Season: End November to end April

Kindergarten: *Non-ski:* from 2½ years. *With ski:* from 2½ years.

Prices: *Lift pass:* 6 days 1,370–1,570 S (children 780–900 S). *Ski school:* Group 1,150 S for 6 days; private 1,650 S per day.

# RATINGS

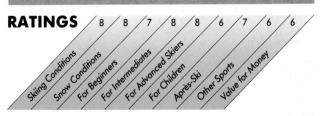

| Skiing Conditions | Snow Conditions | For Beginners | For Intermediates | For Advanced Skiers | For Children | Après-Ski | Other Sports | Value for Money |
|---|---|---|---|---|---|---|---|---|
| 8 | 8 | 7 | 8 | 8 | 6 | 7 | 6 | 6 |

# THE RESORT

If Walt Disney Productions wanted to create an instant traditional ski resort they would model it on this perfect Vorarlberg village with a river running through the middle and sun-kissed slopes on all sides.

Lech owes its exclusive status to comparatively difficult access and high prices. Residents and visitors move with a self-confident, unhurried step, and if the most expensive, up-to-the-minute ski suits are in evidence on the slopes, fur coats are *de rigueur* for the daily promenade at tea time.

# THE SKIING

Lech's skiing links with that of Zürs (5 km. away by road), and the first impression is of perfectly manicured slopes designed to flatter the perfectly manicured, designer-clothed clientele. Closer inspection reveals much tougher work, especially off piste, and the fact that many of the *glitterati* who assemble here each winter are very good skiers.

The village centre is at 1450 m., and a variety of lifts serve the fast, open trails down from the Kriegerhorn and around Oberlech, a satellite settlement perched above the valley. The difficult skiing is beyond, on unpisted ski routes from the Zuger Hochlicht—Lech's highest point at 2377 m.—or down to Zug, a tiny hamlet also on the route back from Zürs via the Madloch-Joch (2438 m) The other return from Zürs, from the top of the Rüfikopf cable car, is another steep, unpisted run. Skiing with a guide, especially after a snowfall, leads to the discovery of bowls and gullies of fresh powder. The 20-km. interlinked Lech-Zürs circuit is perfect for ambitious intermediates who will have to steel themselves for the occasional stern examination of technique.

Lech is at the far end of the Arlberg network of resorts which straddle the Tyrol-Vorarlberg border. The other resorts included on the regional lift pass are St. Christoph, Stuben, Zürs and the most famous ski centre in the region, St. Anton. St. Anton owes a big part of its popularity to being on the railway line and main

road. Getting to Lech requires a little more effort and, its aficionados claim, it is worth it to be away from the crowds who would surely spoil this exclusive winter playground.

At lunchtime, the beautiful, or at least beautifully dressed, people congregate in Oberlech at the bar under a huge red umbrella outside the Sporthotel Petersboden (which also has an indoor restaurant) or in the ancient dining room of the Goldener Berg. Apart from Oberlech's eateries, there isn't much alternative other than skiing back to town or taking lunch at the Palmenalpe restaurant at the top of the chair lift from Zug.

# APRÈS-SKI

Early evening activities can either take the form of shopping for top-quality sportswear, antiques and wood carvings; wandering the streets in the company of couples in matching furs (sometimes, it is rumoured, the family dog will be similarly dressed!); pausing for a hot chocolate or *Jägertee* in the sumptuous lounge of the Gasthof Post, an Alpine institution constructed in sturdy chalet style, stuffed with antiques and famed for impeccable service which appeals to royalty and jet-setters who choose it for their winter sojourn; or taking in the tea dance in the Tannbergerhof.

Unlike its Arlberg neighbour, St. Anton, there is little hubbub in the streets later on but, inside the hotels, there are several good and pricy discos and nightclubs. Taking a sleigh-ride to outlying Zug is a treat, the destination being the Rote Wand, a restaurant-cum-nightclub that is one of the best in the region.

# OTHER ACTIVITIES

The few British operators in Lech organize tobogganing evenings, as well as skating and curling at the small ice rink in the village centre. The *Tenniszentrum* has four indoor courts and two squash courts, and there is a public swimming pool, as well as several in hotels. Cross-country skiers can take advantage of 22 km. along the valley to Zug; walkers have 25 km. of cleared paths. Excursions to Innsbruck are possible by taking a bus to Langen and the train from there.

# LERMOOS

Access: *Nearest airport:* Munich (2 hrs.), Innsbruck (1 hr.). *By road:* A14 motorway to Imst, then over Fernpass. *By rail:* railway station in Lermoos.

Tourist Office: A-6631 Lermoos. Tel. (5673) 24 01

| | |
|---|---|
| Altitude: 1004 m. *Top:* 2118 m. | Ski areas: Grubigstein |
| Language: German | Ski schools: Schischule Lermoos |
| Beds: 3,000 | |
| Population: 900 | Linked resorts: None |
| Health: Doctor in resort. *Hospital:* Reute (20 km.) | Season: December to April |
| | Kindergarten: *Non-ski:* none. *With ski:* 4–15 years. |
| Runs: 22 km. | |
| Lifts: 7 | |

Prices: *Lift pass:* 6 days 1,090 S (children 650 S). *Ski school:* Group 950 S for 6 days; private 320 S per hour.

# RATINGS

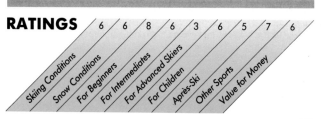

| Skiing Conditions | Snow Conditions | For Beginners | For Intermediates | For Advanced Skiers | For Children | Après-Ski | Other Sports | Value for Money |
|---|---|---|---|---|---|---|---|---|
| 6 | 6 | 8 | 6 | 3 | 6 | 5 | 7 | 6 |

# THE RESORT

The first thing to do on arrival in Lermoos is to stop and take a long look. On a sunny day, the view across the Moos (acres of flat meadowland dotted with tiny huts) to the Zugspitze is truly spectacular.

Beginners constitute the biggest group of visitors to Lermoos and its neighbour across the Moos, Ehrwald. They are separate resorts, although a combined Zugspitze pass can be purchased to cover both of them plus nearby Biberwier, Bichlbach, Berwang and Heiterwang. The pass also allows travel on the local buses and the "Snow Express" railway service, meaning that visiting all of them is easy—the same facility is afforded to holders of the guest card which is issued by hotels to their guests.

The villages are agreeable and friendly without being especially pretty and are a lot less expensive than most Tyrolean centres.

# THE SKIING

Lermoos is served by a single chair lift from each end of the village. They converge at the middle station at 1350 m. where there are occasional queues for a single chair. The section below this point is wide pastureland, ideal for beginners, and the slopes from the top station are excellent for intermediates—long and fast—but most skiers above fourth-year ability will tire of skiing the same runs over again unless they take full advantage of the regional pass and test the other centres nearby.

The other option for a good skier in a party of less accomplished friends is to enrol in one of the special touring classes at the ski school and indulge in tough off-piste exercises, notably down the Gartnertal route from Wolfrathauser. The other favourite route is from just below the Grubigstein (2255 m.) down to the Fernpass.

The ski school is owned by a partnership of instructors who have a vested interest in applying and maintaining the highest standards of tuition and care. Regular guest downhill and cross-country races are organized for visitors.

Ehrwald's skiing is in three sections, none of them close to the village centre. The scenic Ehrwalder Alm is reached by a gondola and is very easy, giving beginners an exceptionally long

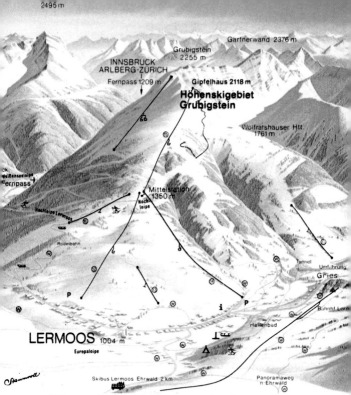

run all the way back to the bottom station. The smallest section, closest to the village, consists of just three drag lifts, but for a different experience altogether, take the Tiroler Zugspitzbahn cable car for the black runs from the middle station or continue the near-vertical journey to the summit (2964 m.)—supplement required—to ski on the German side.

Of the other resorts in the area, Biberwier is closest to the Fernpass and is the most worth visiting. The views of the Tyrol and Bavaria are wondrous and the full range of skiing experiences is

available, albeit in limited supply. If intending to ski on your own, be sure to engage some local knowledge in interpreting the somewhat eccentric piste map.

## APRÈS-SKI

Sleigh-rides on the Moos are seductive on a moonlit evening, fuelled by the inevitable bottle of schnapps proffered by the driver. There are plenty of Tyrolean evenings, as well as party nights consisting of games, beer drinking and yodelling competitions, but the region isn't big on nightlife. The Hotel Tyrol, which doesn't look very special but generates a good atmosphere, is the usual rendezvous at the end of the day's skiing in Lermoos and, after dinner, the Hotel Rustika Tanzcafé's live music/disco evenings attract a good crowd.

## OTHER ACTIVITIES

The Moos provides an enormous flat area for cross-country skiers and walkers. The Hochloipen above both Lermoos and Ehrwald provide much more advanced *Langlauf Loipen*. Ehrwald has indoor tennis courts, and Lermoos features skating and curling plus an indoor sports centre with swimming pool. There is squash in the Hotel Edelweiss.

The most spectacular sight is from the top of the Zugspitze cable car—a magnificent panorama which really gives an on-top-of-the-world feeling as you stand astride the border between Austria and Germany. The railway runs to Garmisch-Partenkirchen where you change for Munich.

# MAYRHOFEN

Access: *Nearest airport:* Munich (2½ hrs.); Innsbruck (1 hr.). *By road:* A12 motorway, exit Wiesing/Zillertal. *By rail:* to Jenbach, then Zillertalbahn or bus.

Tourist Office: A-6290 Mayrhofen. Tel. (05285) 23 05

| | |
|---|---|
| Altitude: 630 m. *Top:* 2250 m. | Ski areas: Ahorn, Penken, Horberg-Gerent |
| Language: German | |
| Beds: 7,700 | Ski schools: Schischule Mayrhofen |
| Population: 3,300 | Linked resorts: Finkenberg |
| Health: Doctors and dentists in resort. *Hospital:* Schwaz (35 km.) | Season: Mid-December to mid-April |
| Runs: 90 km. | Kindergarten: *Non-ski:* 3–12 years. *With ski:* 4–12 years. |
| Lifts: 29 | |

Prices: *Lift pass:* 6 days Zillertal 950–1,160 S (children 700 S). *Ski school:* Group 950 S for 6 days; private 320 S per hour.

# RATINGS

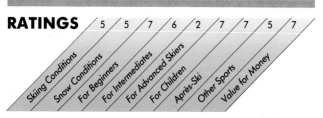

| Skiing Conditions | Snow Conditions | For Beginners | For Intermediates | For Advanced Skiers | For Children | Après-Ski | Other Sports | Value for Money |
|---|---|---|---|---|---|---|---|---|
| 5 | 5 | 7 | 6 | 2 | 7 | 7 | 5 | 7 |

*For map, see p. 83.*

# THE RESORT

Mayrhofen could justifiably claim to be the cradle of British skiing, as its renowned ski school has taught the basics to innumerable children and adults over the last few decades. It is the largest of the Zillertal resorts, connects directly with Finkenberg and links by bus or train with Lanersbach, Hintertux, Zell am Ziller and Fügen—all included on the same lift pass.

Now quite a big town, it has lost much of the Tyrolean character which first attracted tour operators who felt that they could establish a market for good, no-frills ski holidays with excellent tuition and lively nightlife. It is, however, still an excellent place to learn and to enjoy the discos and sleigh-rides.

For better skiers, it is roughly at the mid-point of the valley's resorts, making it the best place from which to explore the Zillertal and Tuxertal.

# THE SKIING

Novices start on the Ahorn mountain immediately to the south of Mayrhofen.

On the other side of town, the Penken ski area has some more demanding slopes. Such is the resort's popularity, the cable cars attract unwieldy queues each morning, a problem which has been partially alleviated by the new lifts around Horberg, which connect with Penken. Waiting for the Ahorn cable car is still something of an ordeal, and although there is a trail all the way back home, it is for advanced intermediates. Beginners, therefore, have to queue again for the cable car back down at the end of the day.

These inconveniences aside, Mayrhofen is always popular with the young set who benefit from painstaking instruction before graduating to uninhibited piste-bashing. The runs down to Finkenberg, home of 1980 Olympic downhill champion Leonhard Stock, offer some challenge, and the glacier at Hintertux guarantees good snow all winter, offset by occasional extreme cold in December and January.

Below the Penken area, the slopes down to the beginning of the new Gerent gondola lift start gently enough, but become quite tricky lower down—beginners beware! A free bus service operates through town between the three lift stations and a six-day pass facilitates use of the train and bus services to neighbouring ski resorts up or down the valley. The children's ski school has an outstanding reputation.

# APRÈS-SKI

Taking tea at the imposing Hotel Elisabeth, near the railway station, is one of the more sedate events in merry Mayrhofen. Nightlife is generally informal and often quite boozy, either at discos (the Andreas Keller, Berghof and Schlüssel are among the liveliest) or when participating in events organized by tour operators. Tyrolean evenings, tobogganing, fondue nights and the weekly ski-school presentation ceremony are all enjoyed by Mayrhofen's predominantly youthful clientele. There are also a few friendly, downbeat bars and restaurants, and a cinema, with films mainly in German.

# OTHER ACTIVITIES

Many hotels have a pool and sauna. There is an indoor public swimming pool, ice-skating, curling on a natural rink, and sleigh-rides, horse riding, tennis in Kantenbach, squash, bowling, and para-gliding are available. A 21-km. cross-country trail takes you to Zell am Ziller, and there are 45 km. of cleared paths for walking in the area.

There are plenty of organized excursions, notably to Innsbruck, Kitzbühel and Salzburg, and Vipiteno and Cortina over the border in Italy. Mayrhofen is the terminus of the Zillertal railway. In summer, a steam locomotive chugs its way along the wide valley to Jenbach, just over an hour's journey. A more prosaic diesel takes its place in winter, but the scenery is just as enthralling. Just before arrival in Jenbach, crane your neck to see the little chapel perched on the cliff to the left. Legend has it that if a girl visited to pray for a husband on three occasions and was still unheeded, she was required to throw herself to the valley floor. Mind you, there are a lot of unlikely legends in this part of Austria! It is also ironic, since nowadays Mayrhofen and its Zillertal neighbours are renowned for providing a boy-meets-girl atmosphere.

# NEUSTIFT/ STUBAI VALLEY

Access: *Nearest airport:* Innsbruck (½ hr.). *By road:* A13 motorway, exit Stubai. *By rail:* to Innsbruck, then by bus.

Tourist Office: A-6167 Neustift. Tel. (05226) 22 28

| | |
|---|---|
| Altitude: 1000 m. *Top:* 3200 m. | Ski areas: Stubai Glacier, Serleslifte, Schlick 2000, Elfter Lifte |
| Language: German | |
| Beds: 6,500 | Ski schools: Schischule Stubaier Gletscher, Schischule Neustift Hochstubai |
| Population: 3,500 | |
| Health: Doctors in Neustift. *Hospital:* Innsbruck (27 km.) | Linked resorts: Mieders, Schönberg, Fulpmes, Telfes |
| Runs: 120 km. in Stubaital | Season: Mid-December to April, all year round on glacier |
| Lifts: 42 in Stubaital | |
| | Kindergarten: *Non-ski:* from 2 years. *With ski:* from 3 years. |

Prices: *Lift pass:* 6 days 1,260 S for Stubaier Glacier area (50% reduction for children under 15 years). *Ski school:* Group 860 S for 5 days; private 300 S per hour.

# RATINGS

| Skiing Conditions | Snow Conditions | For Beginners | For Intermediates | For Advanced Skiers | For Children | Après-Ski | Other Sports | Value for Money |
|---|---|---|---|---|---|---|---|---|
| 5 | 8 | 5 | 6 | 5 | 5 | 5 | 7 | 7 |

*See also map, p. 92.*

# THE RESORT

Twenty minutes from the centre of Innsbruck, the Stubaital satisfies everyone's ideal of the typical Tyrolean valley: lovely, unspoiled villages with onion-domed churches, farmhouses perched precariously above the valley close to high-altitude pastures.

Cosy cafés and old-fashioned hospitality make it the perfect

antidote to high-pressure, high-priced, resorts. The villages, Mieders, Fulpmes, Telfes and Neustift, each have good, but limited, skiing close at hand. Most of the activity is on the Stubai glacier, at the head of the valley, with skiing available throughout the year.

In the summer months the whole valley takes on a new aspect. Sheep and cattle graze by the roadside, fishermen angle for trout, hikers roam the flower-speckled hillsides, and skiers head for the

glacier, 20 minutes from Neustift, fairly sure that they will spend the morning under deep blue skies until the early afternoon sun makes the snow too slushy.

# THE SKIING

Neustift and Mieders each has limited local terrain, with the occasional fright in store for the unwary. Fulpmes and Telfes both have small nursery slopes close to the village centres and share the "Schlick 2000 Skizentrum" which may one day—Alpine politics notwithstanding—be connected with the Innsbruck Olympic Games centre, Axamer Lizum.

It is the Stubai glacier, however, which attracts most visitors to the valley, as it guarantees excellent snow all winter. Even at the end of May conditions are good down to the mid-station. The top station is at 3200 m., from where the views are magnificent, and the upper glacial slopes are gentle—perfect for beginners. Experts will find little challenge unless they opt for race-training weeks in the summer.

# APRÈS-SKI

There is a jolly, but plain, little bar at the bottom of the glacier gondola. Across the car park, the Alpensporthotel Mutterberg is almost a village in itself. Its facilities include indoor pool, sauna, games room, bowling alley and nightclub. Further down the valley, each of the villages has several good bars and places for dancing. None of them are designed to appeal to jet-setters, but all are informal, friendly and less expensive than in better-known resorts. Neustift's Romanstube and Schihaserlkeller both combine good value, uninhibited dancing and a friendly clientele.

# OTHER ACTIVITIES

Mieders and Telfes each has a cross-country *Loipe* just outside, and above Fulpmes and Neustift there are good, long, tree-lined toboggan runs. The sports centre between Fulpmes and Telfes houses an indoor pool and tennis courts with sauna and Turkish baths. Most of the better hotels have good fitness rooms. In

addition, you'll find skibob, skating, curling, bowling, hang-gliding, squash and horse riding in one or other of the villages.

In the summer, after skiing all morning, there are tennis courts and swimming pools, hiking in the hills, free guided walks, and golf at Igls and Seefeld.

The city of Innsbruck is just down the road, and one of the most interesting ways of visiting it is to take the tram which starts in Telfes and meanders its way through Mutters and Natters, before arriving to deposit its mixed cargo of skiers and shoppers in the Tyrolean capital's ancient centre. Another alternative is to drive over the Brenner Pass into Italy. The Europa Bridge is the name given to the motorway perched on massive stilts, which runs to the border. The best way to see it is from the old road in the valley. The contrast between old Tyrol and modern technology is startling.

# NIEDERAU

Access: *Nearest airport:* Innsbruck (1 hr.); Munich (2 hrs.). *By road:* A12 motorway, exit Wörgl-Ost. *By rail:* to Wörgl, then by bus.

Tourist Office: A-6314 Niederau. Tel. (05339) 82 16

Altitude: 828 m. *Top:* 1903 m.

Language: German

Beds: 2,900

Population: 850

Health: Doctor in resort. *Hospital:* Wörgl (7 km.)

Runs: 40 km. in Wildschönau

Lifts: 12 (34 in the Wildschönau)

Ski areas: Markbachjoch, Lanerköpfli

Ski schools: Schischule Wildschönau

Linked resorts: None

Season: Mid-December to mid-April

Kindergarten: *Non-ski:* 3–6 years. *With ski:* from 3 years.

Prices: *Lift pass:* 6 days 1,170 S (children 820 S). *Ski school:* Group 950 S for 6 days (children 15% reduction); private 310 S per hour.

# RATINGS

| Skiing Conditions | Snow Conditions | For Beginners | For Intermediates | For Advanced Skiers | For Children | Après-Ski | Other Sports | Value for Money |
|---|---|---|---|---|---|---|---|---|
| 5 | 6 | 8 | 6 | 4 | 8 | 5 | 5 | 7 |

KITZBÜHELER ALPEN          ZILLERTALER ALPEN

Schweiberghorn 1989 m
Feldalphorn 1920 m
Großer Beil 2309 m
Lämpersberg 2297 m
Joel 1968 m
Salatzberg 1903 m

Schönanger

Lanerköpfl 1600 m
Markbachjoch 1500 m

AUFFACH 870 m

Schönanger

ROGGENBODEN

THIERBACH 1175 m

MÜHLTAL 782 m

OBERAU 936 m

NIEDERAU 828 m

Zauberwinkl

# THE RESORT

Set in the "wild and beautiful valley" of the Wildschönau, Niederau embodies rustic charm and, in common with many other centres in the region, a gentle introduction to skiing and excellent amenities for low-key family holidays, as well as a few treats for experts. Further up the valley, Oberau is a more compact village (with a similarly compact area), and third in the trio is Auffach, at 869 m.

The region is popular with local and German families as well as British tour operators, many of whom offer learn-to-ski packages. For beginners wanting to learn in tranquil surroundings and for multi-generation groups whose requirements range from ski kindergarten to scenic walks in the woods, Niederau and its neighbours are tailor-made.

# THE SKIING

An hourly, free bus service connects the villages, all three covered by the Wildschönau lift pass. Even if the run below the Lanerkopfl chair lift is designated black, it is barely testing for experts unless it has been left untouched, allowing moguls to form. Niederau's skiing is on tree-lined, north-facing slopes whilst those above Auffach face both north and east and are more

exposed at the top. Oberau has but a handful of short drag lifts for novices. Proficient skiers can have a thoroughly good day or two if they concentrate on the Stock run beneath the double chair from the village, the Hochberg FIS downhill course or branch off half way to take the unpisted Katzenberg ski route to Oberau.

There are plenty of off-piste opportunities with a guide, but it is the facility of nursery slopes immediately outside the village, a few lovely tree-lined pistes and views over the Wilder Kaiser and Kitzbüheler Horn which designate Niederau a perfect beginner/intermediate resort.

## APRÈS-SKI

Several bars host a merry throng after skiing, and a programme of evening activities is provided by tour operators. The most popular feature is what the locals, somewhat chauvinistically, claim to be the prettiest sleigh-ride in the Tyrol. It finishes in Penning with lovely views of Hopfgarten and Westendorf en route and culminates in testing a snuff machine and schnapps atomiser amidst much silliness. Tour operators organize fondue evenings, bowling and Tyrolean evenings. On Fridays, the ski school party is a big event in town—prize-giving, dancing and, in the words of the head of the ski school, "so on".

## OTHER ACTIVITIES

Bowling, skating and curling are available in Niederau, tobogganing at Auffach and, 7 km. away in Wörgl, there is indoor swimming and tennis. The cross-country *Loipen* from Niederau reach all the way to Hopfgarten, with some shorter ones close to hand and, far beyond Auffach, where the road peters out, there is another, almost deserted, cross-country route. Cross-country skiers can also ski out to join the sleigh-ride parties and return in comfort after testing the snuff and schnapps devices.

Being up the valley from Wörgl, on a narrow and twisting road, the Wildschönau villages aren't ideal for exploring the Tyrol, although there are organized trips to Berchtesgaden and Salzburg, Innsbruck and Vienna and Vipiteno (Italy) and Munich (Germany), as well as to Venice for the carnival.

# OBERGURGL

Access: *Nearest airport:* Innsbruck (1¼ hrs.); Munich (3½ hrs.). *By road:* A12 motorway, exit Telfs, then via Ötz. *By rail:* to Ötztal, then by bus.

Tourist Office: A-6456 Obergurgl. Tel. (05256) 258

Altitude: 1930 m. *Top:* 3082 m.

Language: German

Beds: 3,040

Population: 350

Health: Doctor in resort. *Hospital:* Zams (70 km.)

Runs: 100 km. in whole area

Lifts: 21

Ski areas: Gaisberg-Hohe Mut, Festkogel, Hochgurgl

Ski schools: Schischule Obergurgl, Schischule Hochgurgl

Linked resorts: None

Season: Mid-November to beginning May

Kindergarten: *Non-ski:* from 3 years. *With ski:* from 5 years.

Prices: *Lift pass:* 6 days 1,250–1,440 S (children 900 S). *Ski school:* Group 950 S for 6 days; private 350–480 S per hour.

# RATINGS

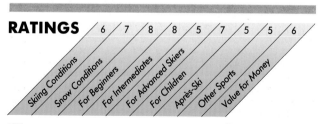

| Skiing Conditions | Snow Conditions | For Beginners | For Intermediates | For Advanced Skiers | For Children | Après-Ski | Other Sports | Value for Money |
|---|---|---|---|---|---|---|---|---|
| 6 | 7 | 8 | 8 | 5 | 7 | 5 | 5 | 6 |

*For map, see p. 196.*

# THE RESORT

At the head of the Ötztal, with the Italian border in sight, Obergurgl's remoteness guarantees its exclusiveness. It is a pretty village and tends to attract the same clientele every year. The cosiness of Obergurgl's hotels and cafés contrasts with the wide-open spaces on the mountainside above.

Sölden is 20 minutes back down the valley and Vent, home of Calgary double-medallist Bernard Gstrein, half an hour's drive, but a separate pass is required for each. Hochgurgl is a more modern settlement high above the valley and is, along with Untergurgl, available on the Obergurgl ticket.

As few tour operators can find accommodation, most visitors have their own cars, convenient for being independent of the free bus service when skiing at Untergurgl or Hochgurgl and for venturing to Vent or Sölden, but presenting difficulties for parking in the twisting, narrow streets.

Austria's highest parish (the village is at 1930 m. and the top station 3082 m.) provides skiing right outside the village, reliable snow and easy, conveniently situated nursery slopes which make it a popular choice for families—some children have inherited the Obergurgl bug from their great grandfathers.

# THE SKIING

Obergurgl's skiing is in two sections which only connect one way, and Untergurgl and Hochgurgl constitute a completely separate resort, linked to Obergurgl by a regular bus service and included on the lift pass.

All of the skiing is above the tree line, apart from the wide, twisting fast trail from Hochgurgl (2150 m.) down to Untergurgl (1793 m.), and has but a handful of difficult runs.

The unpisted ski route down from the Hohe Mut (2670 m.) above Obergurgl, where there is a restaurant whose terrace affords views over the Rotmoos glacier to the Italian border, is the only run down from that point and isn't too difficult if it hasn't been over-skied, but quickly becomes mogul-infested due to being narrow. Another is Hochgurgl's short black trail from the Wurmkogl, and there are a couple more ski routes ending at the bottom of the Festkogllift. There are, however, plenty of opportunities for good skiers if they take the fall line on some of the wider sections which are, in general, of easy-to-intermediate standard.

The tradition of ski touring in the area still attracts more adventurous skiers, and a choice of interesting itineraries, some of them lasting several days, is suggested by the ski school.

Seven restaurants are strategically placed around the mountainsides, all of them at the top or bottom of lifts, and there are plenty more in the villages, notably the terrace of the Hotel Jenewein by the Gaiserberglift in Obergurgl where, on sunny days, skiers break for lunch never to return to the mountain!

Of the neighbouring resorts, Sölden is much larger, with a wide scope on and off piste and should certainly be visited by good skiers for at least a day even though it isn't covered by the same lift pass, while Vent is tiny and only worth a visit for the sake of a change of scene.

## APRÈS-SKI

Obergurgl is blessed with both atmosphere and opportunities for dancing or listening to live music, while Hochgurgl is much quieter (and more expensive), appealing to the crowd for whom skiing is more important than nightlife; Untergurgl is a tiny settlement whose guests usually drive or take the post bus to Obergurgl for an evening out.

The Josl, Gamper and Wiesental cafés are the usual meeting places at the end of the day, while the Edelweiss und Gurgl hosts both tea dances and the end-of-week ski school prize-giving. The Jenewein's disco and live bands at the Edelweiss are complemented by "Fonduedunnit" nights at the Fender—diners at the fondue suppers enact a murder mystery!

## OTHER ACTIVITIES

Some 13 km. of cross-country trails, public swimming pools at the Hotel Hochfirst and Mühle in Obergurgl, a rifle range, skating and curling are among the non-skiing opportunities.

Other than the Ötztaler bus service which calls at all the valley's villages and has the occasional service to Innsbruck, there are few opportunities for exploring.

# OBERTAUERN

Access: *Nearest airport:* Salzburg (1½ hrs.); Munich (2½ hrs.). *By road:* A10 motorway, exit Eben. *By rail:* to Radstadt, then by bus.
Tourist Office: A-5562 Obertauern. Tel. (06456) 252

| | |
|---|---|
| Altitude: 1740 m. *Top:* 2350 m. | Ski areas: Obertauern-Nord, Obertauern-Süd |
| Language: German | |
| Beds: 4,800 | Ski schools: Schischule Obertauern-Nord, Schischule Obertauern-Süd |
| Population: 180 | |
| Health: Doctor in resort. *Hospital:* Tamsweg (40 km.) | Linked resorts: None |
| | Season: December to April |
| Runs: 90 km. | Kindergarten: *Non-ski:* from 3 years. *With ski:* from 3 years. |
| Lifts: 27 | |

Prices: *Lift pass:* 6 days 1,240 S (children 820 S). *Ski school:* Group 950 S for 6 days; private 380 S per hour.

# RATINGS

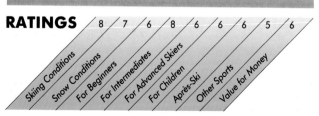

| Skiing Conditions | Snow Conditions | For Beginners | For Intermediates | For Advanced Skiers | For Children | Après-Ski | Other Sports | Value for Money |
|---|---|---|---|---|---|---|---|---|
| 8 | 7 | 6 | 8 | 6 | 6 | 6 | 5 | 6 |

*For map, see pp. 34–35.*

# THE RESORT

The wide main street is evidence that Obertauern was once an important staging post on the old pass through the Tauern Alps. Originally this was the Roman "salt" route between Salzburg and the south; today, the town is bypassed by a modern *Autobahn.*

Anyone looking for a traditional Austrian ski village will be disappointed by the functional exterior. Once inside Obertauern's bars and hotels, however, there is true *Gemütlichkeit:* the discos exude a bop-'til-you-drop atmosphere, and the sports centre recognizes the needs of Austrian, Dutch and German guests, who require a lot more than skiing for winter exercise.

# THE SKIING

Quite simply, it is a bomber's paradise—unless there has been a heavy snowfall when waist-deep waves of powder snow form a sea of pleasure for off-piste aficionados. These extreme conditions are quite common, but Obertauern's recent reputation has been built on a 90-km. pisted circuit which can be skied at full-tilt, in either direction. Breakneck skiing is almost *de rigueur,* and there is plenty to occupy most intermediates.

The lift system has been designed so that there is no need to remove your skis all day, apart from when climbing the steps to the cable car—the head of the ski school delights in demonstrating that even this is possible on skis, but only if he is borrowing someone else's equipment! Better skiers can either enrol in the ski school for off-piste guiding and tuition or, with a car, use the "Top-Tauern-Skischeck".

Obertauern is one of the few towns in Austria where it is possible to ski from and back to your hotel door, with nine access points to the lift system along the main street. There are no hindrances to skiing non-stop all day, should you want. The cafés and restaurants close to the lifts, however, are cosy and enticing.

# APRÈS-SKI

The hard-working Oberhumer family rules the resort. One generation started the ski school, the current one continues it. They manage to combine ski instruction and Austrian music (much of which they have recorded) with running the Gasthof Taverne which attracts an early-evening throng for a sing-song to the accompaniment of guitar and accordion. Huge meat-dominated dinners are fuel for the disco dancing which is unflagging until the early hours. Elsewhere, there are discos with live music, such as the Edelweiss and the Kupferstube in the International.

## OTHER ACTIVITIES

The sports centre has an excellent swimming pool and indoor tennis courts. There is a 7-km. cross-country skiing trail.

Salzburg is 60 km. away. To the south, Villach is a great centre for the pre-Lent *Fasching* carnival.

# SAALBACH-
# HINTERGLEMM

Access: *Nearest airport:* Salzburg (1½ hrs.); Munich (3 hrs.). *By road:* A8 motorway, exit Salzburg, then via Lofer, Maishofen. *By rail:* to Zell am See, then by bus.

Tourist Office: A-5753 Saalbach. Tel. (06541) 72 72

| | |
|---|---|
| Altitude: 1003 m. *Top:* 2097 m. | Ski areas: Schattberg Ost, Zwölferkogel, Kohlmais, Schönleiten, Hochalm, Reiterkogel, Bernkogel |
| Language: German | |
| Beds: 17,000 | |
| Population: 2,500 | Ski schools: Schischule Saalbach, Schi- und Rennschule Hinterglemm, Schischule Mitterlengau |
| Health: Doctors and dentist in resort. *Hospital:* Zell am See (18 km.) | |
| Runs: 180 km. | Linked resorts: Leogang |
| Lifts: 57 | Season: December to April |
| | Kindergarten: *Non-ski:* from 4 years. *With ski:* from 4 years. |

Prices: *Lift pass:* 6 days 1,135–1,420 S (children 705–865 S). *Ski school:* Group 950 S for 6 days; private 380 S per hour.

# RATINGS

| Skiing Conditions | Snow Conditions | For Beginners | For Intermediates | For Advanced Skiers | For Children | Après-Ski | Other Sports | Value for Money |
|---|---|---|---|---|---|---|---|---|
| 9 | 7 | 5 | 10 | 8 | 5 | 9 | 6 | 6 |

# THE RESORT

The old villages, Saalbach and Hinterglemm, have gradually spread out along the Glemm valley to meet each other and have become, after Vienna, Austria's most visited holiday centre. Over 2 million bed nights a year mean that this Salzburgerland resort is a major skiing centre, yet it has been popular until recently only with Austrians and a well-heeled German and Dutch clientele. Now, its huge "Ski Circus"—a 180-km. circuit—and a highly sophisticated nightlife mean that the twin villages appeal to ambitious skiers and high-rollers from all over Europe.

# THE SKIING

The lift system has been cleverly designed to produce some 180 km. of skiing in a pisted circuit skiable in either direction, making following the sun around an easy prospect and providing fast on-piste skiing, as well as endless off-piste forays on both sides of the Glemm valley. As if this isn't enough, Leogang, a little village to the north of the Asitz summit, has its own skiing area and is included on the Saalbach-Hinterglemm lift pass. Kaprun and Zell am See are both a short drive away, but require a separate lift pass.

The Schattberg cable car starts from the middle of Saalbach and rises to 2020 m. where there is a large self-service restaurant with a terrace; it is the main starting point for the circuit to Hinterglemm or, via Jausern, back to Saalbach, with several choices for an off-piste descent. Good skiers can ignore the circuit altogether by taking the Nord trail, an international competition course beneath the cable car, straight back to town.

One problem with Austrian resorts is that although many rightly advertise skiing for all grades, it is in limited supply: not so in this massive, lively and well-maintained centre. The two villages, despite having nearly merged into each other, remain separate entities and each has nursery slopes at its centre and several confidence-boosting long easy trails. Intermediates are able to bash their way around the circuit, fast and furious or calm and collected, as the mood of the day dictates, and if experts tire of exploring all off-piste opportunities, there are several blacker-

147

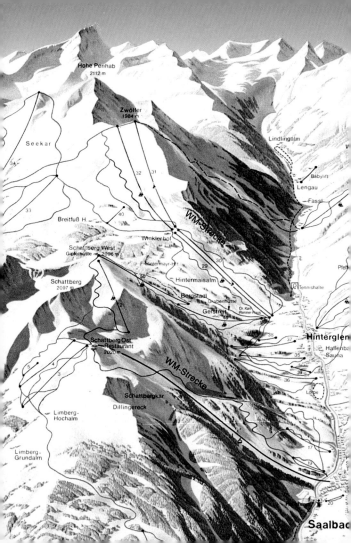

than-black trails which are considered difficult by Austrian standards, let alone those of North European holiday-makers. The Zwölferkogel trail from 1984 m. back to the valley, north-west of Hinterglemm, is generally considered to be one of the most difficult in the region; another international standard circuit starts from the same point.

One of the joys of the region is that, despite the posturing of some of the resorts' guests at the several "ice bars", quite a few old fashioned "huts" are dotted around the mountainsides where you can pop in for a quick coffee, hot chocolate, *Glühwein* or *Jägertee*. One of them is on the way back from the Reiterkogel to Saalbach, where the proprietor delights in taking a pinch of snuff with his guests before sending them on their way. Many misread the piste-markers after this heady experience and find themselves in a farmyard, having to negotiate their way down to the road and taking the bus to the next lift.

There are mountain restaurants a-plenty and, due to the circular design of the lift system, it is always easy to return to the valley. Previously, the only drawback to this magnificent playground was that, being low-lying compared with some better-known places, it could be icy early in the season. Now, artificial snow-making has done a lot to ensure good skiing throughout the winter.

A new 12-person cable car has been added from Vorderglemm to Hochwartalm.

# APRÈS-SKI

Pulsating discos, crowded après-ski bars and one or two quiet cafés make for a lively atmosphere unsuited to a sedate family holiday, but if you want an exciting time, day and night, without the raucousness of some of Austria's cheap'n'cheerful resorts, both villages have a lot to offer.

The Alpenhotel in Saalbach is almost a village in itself, with a quiet lounge overlooking the indoor pool, a merry bar, the rustic Kuhstall tavern featuring traditional music, plus a full-scale nightclub, the Arena, with live band. Its restaurant is one of the best in town. There are plenty of other stylish cafés in town and some pleasant little bars.

## OTHER ACTIVITIES

Many of the larger hotels have indoor pools. There is 20 km. of cross-country skiing along the river bank in Saalbach and further up the valley from Hinterglemm, which has an ice rink next to the *Tennishalle*. The Saalbach sports centre has an indoor pool, tennis courts and bowling alley. Other activities include skibob, sleigh-rides, tobogganing, and walking along 35 km. of cleared paths.

The post bus runs to the head of the valley and on to Zell am See, a sizeable ski resort in its own right with a bustling little town centre and a railway station. It is on the line from Innsbruck to Salzburg, and a day out to either is a fascinating excursion for the journey through the mountains and for shopping or just strolling through the ancient city centres. Closer at hand, there are plenty of quaint old villages, such as Lofer.

# ST. ANTON

Access: *Nearest airport:* Zurich (3½ hrs.); Innsbruck (1½ hrs.). *By road:* A14 motorway to Bludenz. *By rail:* railway station in St. Anton.

Tourist Office: A-6580 St. Anton am Arlberg. Tel. (05446) 22 69 0

Altitude: 1304 m. *Top:* 2650 m.

Language: German

Beds: 7,500

Population: 2,200

Health: Doctors and fracture clinic in resort.
*Hospital:* Landeck (25 km.)

Runs: 300 km. in Arlberg

Lifts: 42 (74 in Arlberg)

Ski areas: Gampen-Kapall, Galzig, Valluga, Rendl

Ski schools: Schischule Arlberg

Linked resorts: St. Christoph, Stuben

Season: End November to end April

Kindergarten: *Non-ski:* 3–14 years. *With ski:* 5–14 years.

Prices: *Lift pass:* 6 days Arlberg Area 1,370–1,570 S (children 780–900 S). *Ski school:* Group 960 S for 6 days; private 1,600 S for 4 hours.

## RATINGS

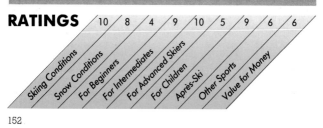

| Skiing Conditions | Snow Conditions | For Beginners | For Intermediates | For Advanced Skiers | For Children | Après-Ski | Other Sports | Value for Money |
|---|---|---|---|---|---|---|---|---|
| 10 | 8 | 4 | 9 | 10 | 5 | 9 | 6 | 6 |

# THE RESORT

Since Hannes Schneider first gave lessons in 1907, St. Anton has been virtually synonymous with Austrian skiing. The cosmopolitan cacophony of American, Japanese and Swedish voices in the cable cars is a testament to its world-wide appeal. Best-known of the Arlberg resorts, it is now quite a large town with the old centre a traffic-free zone.

# THE SKIING

Four main skiing areas of its own (three of them interlinking), a direct connection on skis with Stuben plus the proximity of Lech and Zürs, easily reached by post bus, make St. Anton one of the truly great Alpine centres.

The hub of the area is close to the middle of town, right by the railway station. A funicular railway and parallel chair lift rise to Gampen and thence to the Kapall summit (2326 m.); close by, the Galzig cable car is the starting point for skiing over to St. Christoph or continuing up to the Vallugagrat at 2650 m. Visitors staying at Nasserein, a couple of kilometres to the east, have their own T-bar which connects with the main lift systems, and there is a free shuttle bus to the separate Rendl area—a couple of minutes' ride.

In many respects, St. Anton is best suited to speed-conscious intermediates who revel in fast trails, of which there are dozens, including the motorway-like route from the Ulmerhütte to Rauz and on to Stuben, a tiny village with a sizeable skiing area and a breathtaking off-piste route around the back of the Maroisattel. It requires a bit of uphill work along the way, but is worth it for the experience of breaking fresh powder and sweeping into St. Christoph before pausing to study one's own tracks. Experts relish runs like this and the energy-sapping bumps below Schindler Spitze and beneath the Galzig cable car. Budding downhill racers can test their ability on the Kandahar World Cup course.

For the truly adventurous, strictly with a guide, it is possible to ski the "missing link" of the Arlberg region from the Valluga peak down to Zürs, a half-day adventure which starts with the mind

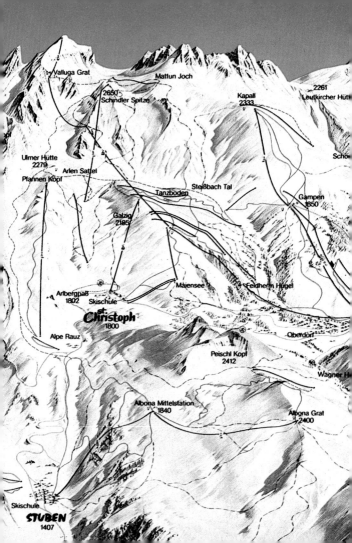

wonderfully concentrated by edging along a ridge to start the descent down an icy wall, culminating in a narrow, rocky gully. The initial terrors over, the pleasure is to be all alone in the high-altitude pastures, too high for animal tracks, before zipping into jet-set Zürs. Another, more expensive, treat is to go with a guide by helicopter, alighting on a cliff-top ledge beyond the Darmstädter Hütte, for another unbroken off-piste run back home.

If all this sounds too daunting to novices, it is true that St. Anton is a serious skier's town but, especially from the top of the Rendl gondola car and above St. Christoph, there is a lot of scope for beginners or timid skiers. Now that the ski school, whose reputation had been dented by accusations of arrogance and over-sized classes, has renewed its traditional zeal in setting the highest standards, St. Anton is a good place to learn or, more particularly, improve. Children can enrol in day-long classes which include games and lunch in the middle of the day and a race every Friday.

St. Anton being high on most skiers' list of resorts to visit, it is inevitable that there are long queues for the main lifts each morning. Two ways of avoiding this congestion are to start the day on the less-crowded Rendl slopes or approach the main lift system from St. Christoph, ten minutes away by bus. The Valluga cable car operates a reservation system, usually allowing time for a quick ski on the Osthang (blue) run prior to taking up one's place.

For a resort of its size, there are few mountain restaurants. The self-service cafés at Gampen, Galzig and Rendl are all large and efficiently run, the last styling itself as the "Rendl Beach" due to a large terrace which takes on a Riviera-like atmosphere on sunny days. It is easy to ski back to St. Anton for lunch. There is a clutch of hotels and restaurants in St. Christoph, and a couple more in Stuben.

The Arlberg lift pass covers St. Anton and St. Christoph—in the Tyrol—and their Vorarlberg neighbours, Stuben, Lech, Zug and Zürs.

# APRÈS-SKI

Après-ski starts early, either in the railway-station bar where ski-bums from around the world congregate to discuss job prospects and swap tales of derring-do, or at the Krazy Känguruh, scene of much Scandinavian merrymaking during "Happy Hour" between 3–4 p.m. in a noisy, verging on riotous, atmosphere. Be careful when skiing home late in the afternoon in this vicinity. Whilst most young Swedes are good skiers, their equilibrium is quickly upset by a tot of schnapps too many.

The famous tea dances in the Hotel Post aren't as sedate as they sound and, as the lifts close, the whole of St. Anton becomes a huge debating theatre, every bar crowded with skiers chewing over the day's activities, tucking into pastries, hot chocolate and *Glühwein*.

Later on, most of the large hotels have discos or dancing to live bands, notably the Stänton in the Sporthotel, very popular with British visitors. There are restaurants to suit all pockets. For a special dinner, take a taxi to St. Christoph where the Arlberg-Hospiz-Hotel is one of the great Alpine hotels.

# OTHER ACTIVITIES

The sports centre near the middle of town has indoor tennis and squash courts. Traditional winter pursuits such as skating, curling, tobogganing at the Rodelhütte, and sleigh-rides are all readily available, plus swimming and bowling. There are 20 km. of cleared walks and 50 km. of cross-country skiing on the opposite side of town from the main lift system and through the trees at the beginning of the Ferwall Valley.

Situated on the main railway line, St. Anton is at the end of the Arlberg tunnel and is well situated for visiting Zurich or the capital of the Tyrol, Innsbruck. Closer at hand, people-watching in trendy Zürs and Lech often results in spotting European royalty and international movie stars.

In town, there is a local history and ski museum, but the best sight of all is from the top of the Valluga cable car—mountains as far as the eye can see.

# ST. JOHANN IM PONGAU

Access: *Nearest airport:* Salzburg (45 mins.); Munich (2½ hrs.). *By road:* A10 motorway, exit St. Johann. *By rail:* railway station in St. Johann.

Tourist Office: A-5600 St. Johann. Tel. (06412) 465

Altitude: 650 m. *Top:* 1850 m.

Language: German

Beds: 3,200

Population: 8,000

Health: Doctors and hospital in St. Johann

Runs: 35 km. (105 km. in 3-Täler-Schischaukel)

Lifts: 17 (60 in 3-Täler-Schischaukel)

Ski areas: Hahnbaum, Gernkogel, Alpendorf

Ski schools: Schischule St. Johann-Alpendorf

Linked resorts: Wagrain, Flachau

Season: Beginning December to end April

Kindergarten: *Non-ski:* none. *With ski:* from 4 years.

Prices: *Lift pass:* 6 days 1,105 S (children 675 S). *Ski school:* Group 340 S per day; private 380 S per hour.

## RATINGS

| Skiing Conditions | Snow Conditions | For Beginners | For Intermediates | For Advanced Skiers | For Children | Après-Ski | Other Sports | Value for Money |
|---|---|---|---|---|---|---|---|---|
| 7 | 6 | 6 | 8 | 5 | 5 | 5 | 6 | 8 |

HOHE TAUERN      Sonnblick

ogel 1787 m

ogel-Alm    Gernkogel

Buchau-Hütte     Stegbachalm

32

Kreisten-Alm

Gernkogel

Sternhof

Alpenhof

Rodelbahn

**ALPENDORF**

800 m

P

Hahnbaum

1200 m

Alm

Schiwanderloipe

Schiwander

35

36

Eislaufplatz

**ST. JOHANN i. P.**

# THE RESORT

Capital of the Pongau region of Salzburgerland, St. Johann isn't the prettiest of resorts. It has a tiny skiing area of its own, perfect for beginners, and, as the major settlement of the "3-Täler" resorts which embrace Alpendorf, Wagrain and Flachau, is an excellent centre for up to intermediate standard. It is a town rather than a village and, unlike most other ski centres in the region, owes its prosperity to light industry, not tourism. That being said, St. Johann has plenty to offer, especially for young budget-conscious skiers.

# THE SKIING

The ski school assembles on Monday mornings with the ebullient promise that if novices haven't learned to ski after six days there will be a full cash refund. The slopes which rise from near the middle of town are excellent for beginners and good for intermediates who want to spend their first day on holiday finding their ski legs. Thereafter, the free bus takes you to Alpendorf each morning, the chosen destination for the roller-coaster runs up and over to Wagrain and on to Flachau.

At the far end of the shuttle *(Schischaukel)*, Flachau's runs tend to be very fast, but not too steep and are recommended for piste-bashers, especially in low season when there is little likelihood of finding resting skiers round a bend. Similarly, the run back home from the Hirschkogel (1755 m.) to Alpendorf (800 m.) can be taken at full tilt. In between, the skiing is similar to that of the Rockies—long runs through trees with very little on piste to deter speed-conscious intermediates.

The "3-Täler" resorts are included on the Top-Tauern-Ski-scheck. Independent ski guides organize excursions; otherwise a car is necessary to explore the region. The ski school has several British instructors.

# APRÈS-SKI

The few British operators which use St. Johann im Pongau organize a full programme of tobogganing, bowling, a visit to the thermal baths at Badgastein, fondue night, an outdoor barbecue in

spring months, and disco nights. There are several nightclubs and bars with dancing in St. Johann and more in Wagrain and Flachau. The younger crowd pack the Ski Lovers pub for party games and impromptu "musical" sessions with a crazy gang of instructors.

## OTHER ACTIVITIES

Indoor tennis and squash (at the Sporthotel Prem, next to the ski lifts), swimming, bowling, tobogganing, skating and curling on natural rinks and walking along cleared paths constitute the sporting options during winter months. Salzburg is an hour away by train.

# ST. JOHANN IN TIROL

Access: *Nearest airport:* Munich (2 hrs.); Salzburg (2 hrs.). *By road:* A12 motorway, exit Kufstein-Süd. *By rail:* railway station in St. Johann.

Tourist Office: A-6380 St. Johann in Tirol. Tel. (05352) 22 18

| | |
|---|---|
| Altitude: 660 m. *Top:* 1700 m. | Ski areas: Harschbichl, Penzing, Eichenhof, Jodelalm, Müllneralm, Buchwies |
| Language: German | |
| Beds: 6,000 | Ski schools: Schischule St. Johann in Tirol |
| Population: 7,000 | |
| Health: Doctors, dentists and hospital in resort | Linked resorts: None |
| | Season: December to March |
| Runs: 50 km. | Kindergarten: *Non-ski:* 2–5 years. *With ski:* 4–12 years. |
| Lifts: 18 | |

Prices: *Lift pass:* 6 days 1,000–1,100 S (children 590–640 S). *Ski school:* Group 340 S per day; private 850 S for half-day.

# RATINGS

| Skiing Conditions | Snow Conditions | For Beginners | For Intermediates | For Advanced Skiers | For Children | Après-Ski | Other Sports | Value for Money |
|---|---|---|---|---|---|---|---|---|
| 6 | 6 | 6 | 8 | 5 | 6 | 7 | 6 | 8 |

# THE RESORT

On the "other" side of the Kitzbüheler Horn from world-renowned Kitzbühel, St. Johann is a bustling and attractive market town. Its slopes are north-facing and, due to climatic conditions around the nearby Wilder Kaiser outcrop, good skiing is guaranteed from December to April in all but the worst winters.

A free shuttle bus connects the village with the main access points, but the centre is only a 10-minute stroll to the gondola station. St. Johann's heroine, Crystl Haas, who won Olympic downhill gold medals in 1964 and 1968, runs the sports shop en route.

Jodla

IX

XIV

Hochfeld 934 m

VIII

XII

V

XIII

XV

I

VII

II

IV

Baumoos P

Bahnhof

P

P

P

P

P

Freizeitzentru

# THE SKIING

With three nursery areas at the bottom of the lift system and plenty
of skiing aloft, to which beginners quickly graduate, St. Johann is
one of Austria's best places in which to learn to ski. Anyone with
more than eight weeks' experience may quickly become bored,
but for intermediates and families there is plenty of scope for long
fast runs through the trees.

Kitzbüheler Horn
2000 m

chbichl 1700 m

Stanglalm

Bergstation Penzing
1463 m

XI Müllneralm

dralm 1200 m

Passegger-
Alm

VI

X

7a

XVI

For ambitious skiers there are few off-piste opportunities; the only challenge is the FIS downhill course to Oberndorf which is used for Austrian National Championship races, but when not prepared for competition, massive moguls form on its two short, steep sections.

Accusations that St. Johann had been resting on its laurels triggered investment in a six-seater gondola from the valley to the resort's highest point, the Harschbichl (1700 m.), replacing the old funicular railway and tripling uphill capacity in the process. There is a new quad-chair up to the Penzing (1463 m.), which has improved connections between the Mullneralm, above Obern-dorf, and the rest of the system. With snow-making apparatus from the Angereralm mid-station all the way back to town installed for the 1988/89 season, St. Johann's status as a good centre for beginners and intermediates is assured.

# APRÈS-SKI

Without being as picturesque as some of its Tyrolean neighbours, St. Johann has a pleasant ambience. Immediately after skiing, the little outdoor bars at the base of its lifts do good business in toting tots of schnapps and dispensing mugs of *Jägertee* or *Glühwein*. Later, the full gamut of après-ski activity is available, ranging from dignified dining to dazzling discos. There are quiet bars, noisy bars, bars with dancing, dancing in discos, dancing to live bands, Tyrolean evenings and sleigh-rides—the full Tyrolean scenario. St. Johann has its own brewery, with a bar on the fourth floor for sampling its output, providing very good views over the village and valley.

# OTHER ACTIVITIES

The sports centre has swimming, sauna, solarium and fitness room, plus indoor tennis courts. Curling (on a natural rink), three bowling alleys, a 2½-km. floodlit toboggan course, an air-rifle range, a riding hall, 74 km. of cross-country trails (courses of tuition available) and 40 km. of winter walking paths make St. Johann perfect for an all-round winter holiday for all ages (your hotel guest card entitles you to reductions).

Ritzy Kitzbühel is only 20 minutes away by road or rail, and the railway offers opportunities to visit Salzburg and Innsbruck independently from the coach excursions which are available. Kitzbühel has a wider variety of shopping, but tourists should note that Kitzbühel's residents tend to visit St. Johann where prices are lower. The most spectacular sightseeing is by plane from the village's airstrip for tours of the Salzkammergut and Salz-burgerland over spectacular Alpine scenery.

# SCHLADMING

Access: *Nearest airport:* Salzburg (1½ hrs.); Munich (3 hrs.). *By road:* A10 motorway, exit Radstadt. *By rail:* railway station in Schladming.

Tourist Office: A-8970 Schladming. Tel. (03687) 22 26 8

| | |
|---|---|
| Altitude: 745 m. *Top:* 2015 m. | Ski areas: Planai, Hochwurzen, Reiteralm |
| Language: German | |
| Beds: 3,400 | Ski schools: Schischule Keinprecht/Kahr |
| Population: 4,000 | |
| Health: Doctors and hospital in resort | Linked resorts: None |
| | Season: Mid-November to end April |
| Runs: 60 km. | |
| Lifts: 24 | Kindergarten: *Non-ski:* none. *With ski:* from 4 years. |

Prices: *Lift pass:* 6 days Dachstein-Tauern area 1,145–1,300 S (children 730–830 S). *Ski school:* Group 350 S per day; private 1,450 S for four hours.

# RATINGS

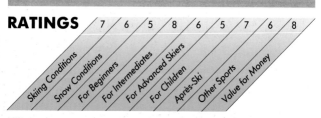

| Skiing Conditions | Snow Conditions | For Beginners | For Intermediates | For Advanced Skiers | For Children | Après-Ski | Other Sports | Value for Money |
|---|---|---|---|---|---|---|---|---|
| 7 | 6 | 5 | 8 | 6 | 5 | 7 | 6 | 8 |

UNTERTAL

OBERTAL

ROHRMOOS

GLEIMING

HOCHWURZEN
1852 m

PREUNEGG

GASSELHÖHE
2001 m

WILDFÜTTERUNG

REITERALM
1860 m

# THE RESORT

A bustling town which, with its neighbour Haus im Ennstal, hosted the 1982 World Championships, Schladming is the largest and best-known resort in Styria. The town centre is dominated by the Protestant and Catholic churches which stand defiantly against each other, producing a distinctive skyline. The old market centre is very pleasant, with a good range of shops. At night, Schladming is very lively, and it is an excellent choice for intermediate skiers who like to be fully occupied, get value for money and explore the other resorts available on the Dachstein-Tauern lift pass.

# THE SKIING

The World Championship men's downhill course on the Planai is famed for being the fastest on the international circuit. That, of course, is when it has been specifically prepared for racing; in ordinary circumstances, the top part is fast enough and easily negotiated by any competent skier, but the final section is treacherous, mogul-infested and steep. Otherwise, there is little that is really challenging on piste, nearly all the marked trails being well maintained with some lovely tree-lined routes for beginners.

The extra pleasure for good skiers is trying out the other resorts available on the regional lift pass. Reiteralm (1860 m.) is another mountain above the small resort of Pichl, ten minutes away from Schladming by bus. Its skiing is similar to that of Rohrmoos—wide, swooping pistes, mostly through the trees,

marvellous views from the top station and friendly mountain restaurants. Haus im Ennstal, to the east and dominated by the Hauser Kaibling ski area at 2115 m., is larger, having hosted the women's events in 1982. All are reached by the local bus service, and most tour operators include days out in their weekly schedule.

Having a car makes it possible to use another lift ticket—the Top-Tauern-Skischeck—which includes those resorts in the immediate vicinity of Schladming, as well as the other smaller Styrian centres nearby, plus another dozen or so Salzburgerland centres within 30 minutes' drive. This means that it is possible to have several days out in a fortnight's holiday using Schladming as a base. This does not mean that Schladming's own skiing is inadequate—far from it. There is more than enough for good recreational skiers, but it's nice to know that there is even more variety close at hand.

## APRÈS-SKI

Nightlife in Schladming can be formal at hotels like the Alte Post, where there are several dining rooms, ranging from grand to folksy, or jolly bars like the Talbachschenke ("Valley Brook Inn"), where multilingual singsongs are great fun in the cavernous tavern which provides good, basic meals. There are also plenty of ordinary bars and several places with dancing.

## OTHER ACTIVITIES

At Haus, there is an excellent toboggan run on the Hauser Kaibling used by tour operators for *Glühwein* parties. The locals preach the philosophy of being close to nature by providing excellent networks of cross-country trails (25 km.); curling and skating, swimming, tennis, squash and bowling are all available. There are 50 km. of winter footpaths, sleigh-rides and nature excursions to observe the local wildlife.

Graz, historic capital of Styria, is several hours drive away. Should the weather be too bad for skiing or you just want a break, a visit to Salzburg (40 minutes by train) provides an eye-opening insight into one of Europe's classic cities.

# SCHRUNS/ MONTAFON

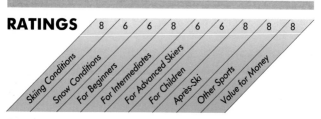

*Access: Nearest airport:* Zurich (2 hrs.). *By road:* A14 motorway to Bludenz. *By rail:* railway station in Schruns.

Tourist Office: A-6780 Schruns/Montafon. Tel. (05556) 21 66

| | |
|---|---|
| Altitude: 700 m. *Top:* 2400 m. | Lifts: 73 in Montafon Valley |
| Language: German | Ski areas: Hochjoch, Seebliga, |
| Beds: 3,800 | Ski schools: Schischule Schruns |
| Population: 3,900 | Linked resorts: None |
| Health: Doctors in Schruns. *Hospital:* Bludenz (13 km. from Schruns). | Season: Mid-December to end April |
| Runs: 206 km. in Montafon Valley | Kindergarten: *Non-ski:* from 3 years. *With ski:* from 3 years. |

Prices: *Lift pass:* 6 days Montafon Valley 1,215–1,410 S (children 765–870 S). *Ski school:* Group 1,100 S for 5 days; private 400 S per hour.

# RATINGS

| Skiing Conditions | Snow Conditions | For Beginners | For Intermediates | For Advanced Skiers | For Children | Après-Ski | Other Sports | Value for Money |
|---|---|---|---|---|---|---|---|---|
| 8 | 6 | 6 | 8 | 6 | 6 | 8 | 8 | 8 |

# THE RESORTS

The Montafon ("Valley in the Mountains") has twelve villages with accommodation and five resorts, none of them especially big but which, combined, amount to a magnificent ski region. The area has been virtually undiscovered by the British tour operators who concentrate on the Tyrol and Salzburgerland. Judicious use of the efficient post bus service means that it is possible to take full advantage of the lift pass and other amenities, although having a car gives more flexibility.

Each of the five villages is a good centre in its own right and satisfies a variety of requirements: Gargellen, with a population of just 100, three four-star hotels and an international clientele, is the best choice for an elegant winter holiday; Gaschurn and St. Gallenkirch share the Silvretta Nova which has the biggest lift system and variety of runs for good skiers; Schruns is the liveliest, with good bars, clubs and shopping but is less atmospheric; Tschagguns is midway between Schruns and Gargellen in terms of style, was one of the Vorarlberg's original resorts, has most of its accommodation in *Gasthöfe* and private homes and is the home of Anita Wachter, whose gold medal at the Calgary Olympics brought enormous pride to the whole Montafon region.

Hard by the border with Swiss Graubünden, the local dialect is tinged with traces of the old Romansh language, the first settlers having arrived from Switzerland early in the 15th century, building a chapel in Gargellen in 1411—St. Gallenkirch's church was founded in 1254, Celtic monks having established Christianity in the region. Pastoral farming and iron works were the Montafon's early industries but today tourism is the lifeblood.

It says a lot for the skiing and quality of accommodation in the Montafon that one of the biggest groups of visitors is the discerning Swiss. To be as central as possible in the Montafon, stay in St. Gallenkirch.

# THE SKIING

It would be easiest to condemn Gargellen for having the smallest and easiest skiing terrain were it not for the off-piste and touring opportunities, notably over the Swiss border to Klosters and back, a mission which the locals are keen to point out has been

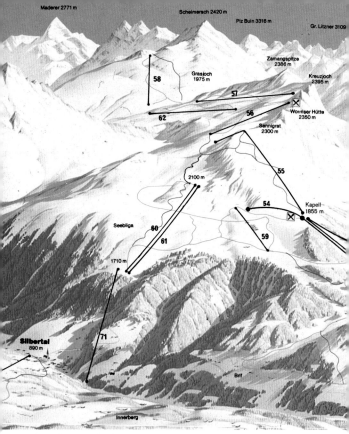

undertaken by the Prince of Wales. Exposed at the top (2150 m.) and wooded lower down, the piste skiing is undemanding and very pretty, leading back to the door of the Hotel Madrisa which is a sophisticated pit stop at the end of the day.

Both St. Gallenkirch and Gaschurn have gondola systems and share (no doubt for the sake of harmony) a top station listed as

2200 m. St. Gallenkirch's skiing is below the Valiseraspitze and that of Gaschurn the Silvretta Nova—their lift systems meet in the Alpe Nova valley. Just about every type of skiing is to be found except long, difficult trails for experts, but the off-piste sections are superb. The Hochjoch has a cable car running from near the centre of Schruns and a gondola from just outside town serving

easy to intermediate skiing. Tschagguns, which has been host to several ladies' World Cup races, as befits the home of Ms. Wachter, is north-facing and has a two-stage funicular railway plus the option of taking a two-seater chair and then the super-fast four-seater to above the tree line, from where the views are staggering. Fast on-piste skiing is the name of the game here. As well as four separate areas with a total of 73 lifts and 206 km. of marked trails, the Montafon offers para-skiing, heli-skiing beyond Parthenen at Bielerhöhe and ski-school tours to Klosters and Galtür.

# APRÈS-SKI

Each of the resorts has bars for a drink at the end of the day, but nightlife in general is not designed to appeal to the wild crowd who flock to better-known places in the Tyrol. These Vorarlberg villages do have their high spots, however, notably the Chaverna disco beneath the Hotel Madrisa in Gargellen. The better hotels frequently have live music, with the occasional jazz combo as a supplement to the usual fare of standard international or Austrian regional music.

Schruns has a couple of lovely old coffee houses in addition to several good hotel restaurants; the Altmontafon in Gaschurn (specializing in Vorarlberg fruit and fish), and game dinners at the Heimspitze draw an eager crowd of diners from as far away as Bludenz.

# OTHER ACTIVITIES

Schruns, Tschagguns and Gaschurn each has indoor tennis courts—the first two share artificial rinks for skating and curling and there is a natural one in Gaschurn. The only swimming pool open to the public is in the Hotel Löwen (Schruns) but 13 others have pools for their guests, most of them with the usual health facilities such as sauna and massage. Ten hotels have bowling, and the Sporthotel Grandau in St. Gallenkirch features a squash court.

The best of the tobogganing is at Tschagguns—a 3-km. floodlit course runs between Latschau and Vanduns, whilst the organizers of the run from the Hotel Botle at Ziegerberg issue helmets with lamps for evening descents.

Though not a major feature of the region, the 110 km. of cross-country *Loipen* provide a few treats, such as the 15-km. circuit on the frozen Silvretta lake (up at 2000 m.) and the panoramic 11-km. trail above Kristberg, beyond Silbertal from Schruns.

The railway station in Schruns connects with Bludenz and thence Zurich, St. Anton and Innsbruck. By car, Feldkirch, Bregenz (where there is a casino), Liechtenstein, St. Anton, Lech and Swiss resorts such as Davos and Lenzerheide are easily accessible.

# SEEFELD

Access: *Nearest airport:* Innsbruck (½ hr.); Munich (1½ hrs.). *By road:* A12 motorway, exit Zirl-Ost. *By rail:* railway station in Seefeld.

Tourist Office: A-6100 Seefeld. Tel. (05212) 23 13

| | |
|---|---|
| Altitude: 1200 m. *Top:* 2074 m. | Lifts: 17 |
| Language: German | Ski areas: Rosshütte, Gschwandtkopf, Geigenbühel |
| Beds: 8,500 | |
| Population: 2,600 | Ski schools: Schischule Seefeld |
| Health: Doctors and dentists in resort. *Hospital:* Innsbruck (25 km.) | Linked resorts: Reith |
| | Season: December to March |
| Runs: 25 km. | Kindergarten: *Non-ski:* from 4 years. *With ski:* from 4 years. |

Prices: *Lift pass:* 6 days 1,090–1,280 S (children 820–960 S). *Ski school:* Group 950 S for 6 days; private 300 S per hour.

# RATINGS

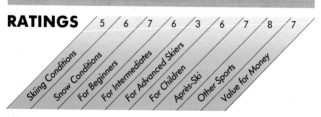

| Skiing Conditions | Snow Conditions | For Beginners | For Intermediates | For Advanced Skiers | For Children | Après-Ski | Other Sports | Value for Money |
|---|---|---|---|---|---|---|---|---|
| 5 | 6 | 7 | 6 | 3 | 6 | 7 | 8 | 7 |

# THE RESORT

The usual cliché is that Seefeld, set on a sunny plateau near Innsbruck, is a world-renowned *Langlauf* centre with a token amount of downhill skiing. This does the resort an injustice. Despite being far removed from top status as a ski resort, Seefeld is one of the best places in Europe for an all-round winter sports holiday, especially for senior skiers who have turned from Alpine to cross-country skiing and who value their creature comforts, as well as for family and beginner groups who enjoy the après-ski and other sports facilities as much as skiing itself.

A large village, efficiently run but short on rustic *Gemütlichkeit,* Seefeld has dozens of hotels with sauna and other health facilities, public and private swimming pools, a pedestrian zone with antique, clothing and souvenir shops; it is, however, quite pricey. Nightlife is as sedate or lively (and late) as required, and to gauge the attitude of visitors from Germany and Holland, note that many strap both Alpine and nordic skis to their cars, as well as packing swimsuits and walking boots to take full advantage of Seefeld's multifarious facilities. They also take a jacket and tie or smart dresses for eating in the better restaurants and visiting the casino.

But if this makes Seefeld sound rather grand, it isn't. Far removed from Lech or Ischgl in terms of style, it is genuinely a resort for all tastes, with a long-standing reputation as a place to learn and develop ski technique despite being best known as the centre for nordic events at the 1964 and 1976 Olympics and hosting the World Championships for the first time in 1985.

# THE SKIING

There are three separate areas connected by a free bus service. The Geigenbühel beginner slopes by the village centre are sardonically known as Idiots Hill by jaundiced tour operator reps. The Gschwandtkopf is for fast-learning beginners to moderate intermediates, and the Rosshütte has some proper grown-up skiing with a mountain railway and two cable cars, as well as a network of drag lifts for good to advanced skiers.

It would be quite wrong to recommend Seefeld to an avid expert, but the run down from the Härmelekopf (2050 m.) is a dream for budding downhillers. It can only be reached by a

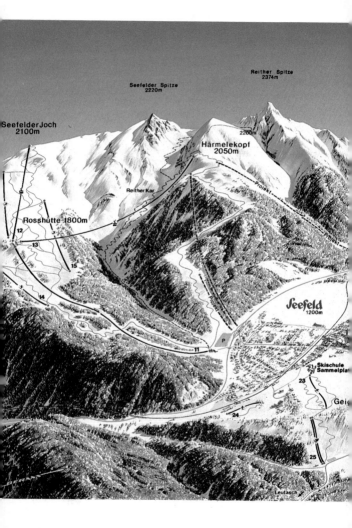

Kalkkögel            Hocheder

Axamer Lizum

Gschwandtkopf
1500m

Innsbruck

29

30

Reith

5

P

8

28

Seewaldalm

3

4

1   2    6

Sprungstadion

Sport- und
Kongreßzentrum

P

7

WM-Halle
Parkgarage

Wildmoosalm

25-person cable car from the top of the railway so that it is always uncrowded and, being well pisted, satisfies the needs of any embryonic Klammer, Müller or Zurbriggen. For real experts, there are some steep off-piste routes from the Reither Kar, although they should only be explored with a guide.

Leutasch is 7 km. away and covered by the same pass—a small area, only worth visiting for a change of scene. Even smaller, Mosern is 5 km. in the opposite direction, but a separate pass is required. Just two T-bars comprise the uphill transportation, but it is a quiet alternative if you have young children and are happy to potter about on the same easy slopes all day.

# APRÈS-SKI

Tea dances to the accompaniment of live bands in the Hotels Kaltschmid (which claims to have the largest bar in Austria), Klosterbräu, Tyrol and igloo-shaped Siglu kick off the evening's entertainment in rollicking style. The Britannia, which is much as you would expect, serves fish and chips; in contrast there is Tyrolean music featuring yodelling duets or zither in the Bräukeller in the Hotel Klosterbräu.

The shops in the pedestrian zone offer a higher standard of antiques and local crafts than is usually found in ski resorts. Seefeld's casino provides 200 schillings of gambling chips in return for the 170 schillings entry fee (jacket, tie and passport required) and the hotels mentioned above have dancing to live bands after dinner, augmented by discos at the Post and Drop In which are less expensive and cater to the younger crowd.

Organized events such as fondue evenings and games nights are provided by tour operators, and Seefeld sometimes seems awash with horse-drawn sleighs, not surprisingly as the gently rolling surrounding countryside lends itself to leisurely exploration by day or night.

# OTHER ACTIVITIES

The big event in Seefeld, cross-country skiing, has 200 km. of mechanically prepared trails with the full range between easy *Loipen* for beginners (hire-equipment and excellent tuition

available) to tough runs for Olympians, all starting from the town's Sports and Congress Centre. Bowling, curling, skating, tennis, swimming and tobogganing are ingredients in Seefeld's mix of non-skiing activities.

As Seefeld is only 10 minutes from the Inn valley, there is limitless opportunity for touring the surrounding region by road—car hire is available in the village. Alternatively, Seefeld is on the railway line between Innsbruck and Garmisch-Partenkirchen in Bavaria, from where connections can be made to Munich.

# SERFAUS

Access: *Nearest airport:* Innsbruck (1 hr.); Munich (4 hrs.). *By road:* A14 motorway to Bludenz, then via Landeck and Ried. *By rail:* to Landeck, then by bus.

Tourist Office: A-6534 Serfaus/Tirol. Tel. (05476) 62 39

---

Altitude: 1427 m. *Top:* 2745 m.

Language: German

Beds: 3,800

Population: 900

Health: Doctor in resort. *Hospital:* in Zams (30 km.)

Runs: 40 km.

Lifts: 19

Ski areas: Lazid, Masner, Alpkopf

Ski schools: Schischule Serfaus-Komperdell

Linked resorts: Fiss, Ladis

Season: Mid-December to April

Kindergarten: *Non-ski:* from 2 years. *With-ski:* from 4 years.

Prices: *Lift pass:* 6 days 940–1,310 S (children 510–605 S). *Ski school:* Group 950 S for 6 days; private 400 S per hour.

---

# RATINGS

| Skiing Conditions | Snow Conditions | For Beginners | For Intermediates | For Advanced Skiers | For Children | Après-Ski | Other Sports | Value for Money |
|---|---|---|---|---|---|---|---|---|
| 5 | 6 | 6 | 6 | 3 | 6 | 6 | 5 | 5 |

# THE RESORT

On a sunny plateau in the Samnaun mountains of the Tyrol, Serfaus had become so popular with its predominantly well-heeled Dutch and German clientele that their cars were in danger of either choking or mowing down pedestrians. So the village fathers took the bold decision to build an underground railway between a car park at one end of the village and the lift system at the other. Now, with access to traffic strictly limited, the streets of the pretty village are safe for walking and, if your hotel is conveniently situated, skiing home at the end of the day. The Dorfbahn has two stops in the village, making Serfaus an especially hassle-free resort.

A mixture of 16th-century barns, two small churches and chalet-style houses and hotels make a traditional Tyrolean scenario. Perched on a ledge above the Inn valley, Serfaus is perfect for couples and families for whom a civilized atmosphere is as important as magnificent views and largely undemanding skiing. Standards of accommodation are particularly high—so are the prices—and if you really want to be pampered, the Cervosa and Löwen are the best hotels.

# THE SKIING

There is a separate nursery area immediately above the village which can be skied to from the main section, making it easy for groups of mixed ability to meet for lunch or to rendezvous in one of the hotels for a tea dance at the end of the day. A choice of

gondola or cable car takes skiers to the Kölner Haus mid-station where there are three especially good restaurants; alternatively, take the chair lift to Alpkopf (2012 m.). From these points, the lift system fans out to either Plansegg (2365 m.), from where there is a long, wide trail suitable for fast intermediates, or Lazid (2351 m.), which is the starting point for some testing skiing nearby, as well as the easy routes to and from the highest point in the Serfaus area—the Zandersjoch at 2745 m.

The lower slopes are tree-lined and therefore protected from the wind, but in the open area above it can be bitterly cold in the depths of winter. In spring, however, one would be unlucky not to enjoy long sunny days amidst spectacular scenery. In all, there are 40 km. of marked trails.

Better skiers enjoy the more limited area of Fiss which may, one day, be completely connected with Serfaus but is currently linked one way only—the return journey.

## APRÈS-SKI

Serfaus seems positively to discourage the young and lively set with quite high prices and a rather genteel atmosphere, but that's not to say that it's difficult to enjoy yourself. Tea dances may sound old hat, but the early evening knees-up in several places around town is an enjoyable interlude between the skiing and relaxing in the sauna and Jacuzzi which are standard facilities in most hotels, the better ones featuring a pool. After dinner there are plenty of opportunities for dancing to traditional Austrian music and the latest disco sounds.

## OTHER ACTIVITIES

There are cleared paths for walking, a lovely network of cross-country trails on the plateau between Serfaus and Fiss, curling, ice-skating and tobogganing.

Serfaus has a history dating back to 1500 B.C., and although summertime is best for examining the ancient Roman remains, there are several close to the village which can be visited during the ski season. Further afield, you can visit Innsbruck by taking a taxi to Landeck and then a train.

# SÖLDEN

Access: *Nearest airport:* Innsbruck (1 hr.); Munich (4 hrs.). *By road:* A14 motorway to Imst, then via Ötz. *By rail:* to Ötztal or Innsbruck, then by bus.

Tourist Office: A-6450 Sölden. Tel. (05254) 22 12 0

Altitude: 1377 m. *Top:* 3058 m.

Language: German

Beds: 8,261

Population: 2,400

Health: Doctors and fracture clinic in resort.
*Hospital:* Zams (70 km.)

Runs: 101 km.

Lifts: 23, plus 10 on glacier

Ski areas: Sölden, Hochsölden, Gaislachkogl

Ski schools: Schischule Sölden-Hochsölden

Linked resorts: Hochsölden

Season: Mid-December to mid-April

Kindergarten: *Non-ski:* 3–8 years. *With ski:* 3–8 years.

Prices: *Lift pass:* 6 days 1,330–1,520 S (children 920 S). *Ski school:* Group 950 S for 6 days; private 340 S per day.

# RATINGS

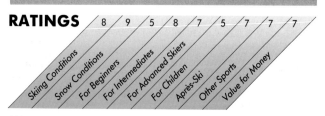

| Skiing Conditions | Snow Conditions | For Beginners | For Intermediates | For Advanced Skiers | For Children | Après-Ski | Other Sports | Value for Money |
|---|---|---|---|---|---|---|---|---|
| 8 | 9 | 5 | 8 | 7 | 5 | 7 | 7 | 7 |

# THE RESORT

With the Gaislachkogl (3058 m.) flanked by two glaciers, Sölden is a year-round skiing centre. If the town's first appearance is a little less than enchanting, its hotels, après-ski bars and nightclubs quickly persuade visitors that, in addition to being one of Austria's better skiing areas, Sölden is also one of the country's better all-round resorts. Hochsölden is perched above the Ötztal valley and, consisting of half-a-dozen hotels and a couple of shops, is the choice for serious skiers who like to be able to ski from and back to their hotels each day and are content to enjoy a low-key atmosphere in the evening. Sölden's atmosphere is far from low-key and for all-round quality ranks at the top of the second division of Austrian ski centres.

The Ötztal runs from near Imst in the Inn valley and peters out at Obergurgl (20 minutes drive away from Sölden), for which a separate lift pass is required. The valley's new hero is Olympic silver medallist Bernard Gstrein whose exploits in Calgary prompted exuberant celebrations throughout the area, most of all in Vent, his home, a tiny ski village tucked in beneath the Wildspitze (3774 m.).

Sölden is for active people and should be shunned by anyone looking for a gentle winter holiday. There are few truly traditional bars in the centre of the sprawling village (although there are several dotted around hillsides in hamlets such as Innerwald), but dancing, drinking and chatting continues all night.

The clientele is international, and a high standard of accommodation and restaurants reflects the fact that most visitors make their own arrangements.

# THE SKIING

Sölden's ski school has been the regular winner of the Austrian instructors' championships, and with a high-season staff of 200 (80% of them English-speaking), there is full scope for everyone from novice to expert. The old cable car at the southern end of the village is being demolished to make way for a 24-person gondola for the 1988/89 season and will increase the uphill capacity from that point to 2,600 people per hour.

Despite Sölden's high altitude, all of the main runs home have

snow-making equipment; in contrast, there is skiing on both glaciers—linked by a road tunnel through the mountains—year-round, although overabundant snow may cause it to close for periods between Christmas and March.

The skiing is in two sections which meet in the Rettenbach valley. The northern sector is shared by Hochsölden (2090 m.), and access from Sölden is by four-seater gondola with an adjacent chair lift linking the two villages.

Early-risers staying in Hochsölden leap on their skis first thing in the morning and choose between a blue or black run down to the base of the gondola in readiness for its first ascent at 8 a.m. Both routes can be crowded at the end of the day and are at their best during the first couple of hours in the morning when most other skiers are concentrating on the higher slopes.

There is a large self-service restaurant, with waitress service upstairs, near the middle station, but the steamy Eugen's Obstlerhütte below Hochsölden has more *Gemütlichkeit* appeal— a favourite pit stop for drinks as well as lunch.

The southern section will be served by the new 24-person

gondola and, as well having the exciting long red trail from the Gaislachkogl restaurant all the way to the valley, has a sprinkling of black runs, notably the steep Wilde Abfahrt ski route which starts from the same point.

## APRÈS-SKI

In addition to the hotels and a couple of noisy but friendly outdoor bars in the main street, which do a quite literally roaring trade in the late afternoon, elegant cafés such as the Carola are the scene of civilized conversation and the quiet sipping of hot chocolate. The evening atmosphere is carefree, whether in bars, discos or several nightclubs with live bands.

## OTHER ACTIVITIES

The sports centre features an indoor swimming pool (with a separate children's section), tennis courts, two large saunas, five solarium rooms, massage, table tennis, bowling and a rifle range.

Bowling evenings at the Park Hotel organized by British tour operators are convivial, as are the tobogganing nights which entail being driven to the Silbertal restaurant for bouts of drinking and singing before an occasionally perilous 4½-km. descent— there is music from 8.30 p.m. until 1 a.m. and the multinational crowd are able to grill their own chops at the indoor barbecue.

There is limited cross-country skiing, but a popular evening diversion is to go by taxi to Zwieselstein for a bonfire party before taking the *Langlauf* trail back again. Curling and skating on a natural rink are available, weather permitting. The Ötztal is a well-known area for serious rock- and ice-climbers in spring and summer.

Excursion possibilities are negligible, although the Ötztaler bus service runs to as far away as Innsbruck. Otherwise, the local buses run to Obergurgl, a pretty village with several restaurants with terraces overlooking the slopes.

# SÖLL

Access: *Nearest airport:* Munich (1½ hrs.). *By road:* A12 motorway, exit Wörgl-Ost. *By rail:* to Kufstein, then by bus.

Tourist Office: A-6306 Söll. Tel. (05333) 52 16

| | |
|---|---|
| Altitude: 703 m. *Top:* 1829 m. | Ski areas: Söll, Hoch-Söll |
| Language: German | Ski schools: Schischule Söll Embacher |
| Beds: 3,500 | |
| Population: 2,700 | Linked resorts: Scheffau, Ellmau, Going, Itter, Hopfgarten, Brixen |
| Health: Doctor in resort. *Hospital:* Wörgl or Kufstein (13 km.) | |
| Runs: 35 km. (200 km. Wilder Kaiser-Brixental) | Season: December to April |
| | Kindergarten: *Non-ski:* none. *With ski:* 5–14 years. |
| Lifts: 13 (86 Wilder Kaiser-Brixental) | |

Prices: *Lift pass:* 6 days 945 S (children 580 S), Skigrossraum Wilder Kaiser-Brixental 1,140 S (children 665 S). *Ski school:* Group 950 S for 6 days; private 230 S per hour.

## RATINGS

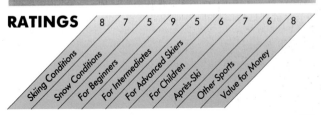

| Skiing Conditions | Snow Conditions | For Beginners | For Intermediates | For Advanced Skiers | For Children | Après-Ski | Other Sports | Value for Money |
|---|---|---|---|---|---|---|---|---|
| 8 | 7 | 5 | 9 | 5 | 6 | 7 | 6 | 8 |

# THE RESORT

Söll is instant Tyrol. Pleasing to the eye, lively and welcoming, its attractiveness and competitive prices make it a favourite destination for young Britons seeking non-stop action, day and night. Value for money is Söll's stock in trade. If you are looking for a little more sophistication, choose one of Söll's neighbours, such as Scheffau or Ellmau which, along with Going, Itter, Hopfgarten and Brixen, share the Skigrossraum Wilder Kaiser-Brixental.

There are some top-quality hotels in Söll, too, notably the 13th-century Gasthof Post and its modern cousin next door, the Hotel Post, which stand out as oases of civilized charm amid the merry bustle all around.

# THE SKIING

The famed ski school makes Söll a particular favourite for beginners or improving intermediates—the nursery slopes at the base of the lift system do not require a lift pass. There are more than enough on-piste opportunities for good skiers (86 lifts and over 200 km. of piste in the Skigrossraum). Pretty Westendorf, whose lifts do not connect with the rest of the system, is included on the Skigrossraum pass and is well worth a day's excursion (ski to Brixen and take the free bus). The pleasure for intermediates is to set off each day choosing Brixen or Hopfgarten as destinations via the Hohe Salve (1829 m.), where there is a little chapel, smart self-service restaurant and, on sunny days, top-of-the-world views over the entire region, including Westendorf immediately below and Kitzbühel in the far distance. Alternatively, there are several descents to Itter, Scheffau, Ellmau and Going, all of which can also be reached by post bus or taxi.

There are two, unavoidable bottlenecks around the Skigrossraum's "spaghetti junction" of lifts and pistes, but the whole area is an intermediate's dream. (A tip, if you want to get to Scheffau or Ellmau quickly, is to branch off to the Innerkert cable car rather than continuing up and over the Hohe Salve.) For fast skiing there are some excellent routes, notably the red run down to the bottom of Itter's new triple chair: it is usually uncrowded and a good intermediate feels like a champion downhill racer.

The weekly visitors' races under the BRISTAR and WiSBI schemes add a competitive edge, and the ski school has its own races, with an evening's prize-giving party.

## APRÈS-SKI

Every night is party night in Söll. There are surprisingly few bars for a resort with such an ebullient reputation, but those which exist are boisterous and, it must be said, sometimes rowdy—but no more so than some in smart Kitzbühel. The traditional meeting place at the end of the day is the Post's ancient, cavernous tavern bar, while the Whiskymühle and the Hotel Tyrol's Dorfstadl discos throb on until the last customers flop into the streets, and tour operators pack guests into Tyrolean evenings featuring *Lederhosen*, wood chopping, thigh slapping and all the attendant high jinks, as well as organizing fondue nights, and family evenings which include bowling, with prizes and forfeits of schnapps (for the adults!).

## OTHER ACTIVITIES

The illuminated toboggan run from Hochsöll to the base of the lift system is popular, as is the swimming pool. There is a natural ice rink, and sleigh-rides round the village are possible.

The main excursions are to Berchtesgaden and Salzburg, the wildlife park at Aurach, Kufstein (with a stop at the Riedl glass factory), Innsbruck and Vipiteno (over the Italian border via the Brenner Pass).

# WESTENDORF

Access: *Nearest airport:* Munich (2½ hrs.); Innsbruck (1 hr.). *By road:* A12 motorway, exit Wörgl-Ost. *By rail:* railway station in Westendorf.

Tourist Office: A-6363 Westendorf. Tel. (05334) 62 30

---

Altitude: 800 m. *Top:* 2000 m.

Language: German

Beds: 4,000

Population: 2,950

Health: Doctors and dentist in resort. *Hospital:* Kitzbühel (15 km.), Wörgl (17 km.)

Runs: 40 km. (210 km. in Wilder Kaiser-Brixental)

Lifts: 14 (86 in Wilder Kaiser-Brixental)

Ski areas: Gampenkogel, Fleiding, Choralpe

Ski schools: Schischule Westendorf

Linked resorts: None

Season: Mid-December to April

Kindergarten: *Non-ski:* from 2 years. *With ski:* from 4 years.

---

Prices: *Lift pass:* 6 days 1,040 S (children 620 S). *Ski school:* Group 340 S per day; private 320 S per hour.

# RATINGS

| Skiing Conditions | Snow Conditions | For Beginners | For Intermediates | For Advanced Skiers | For Children | Après-Ski | Other Sports | Value for Money |
|---|---|---|---|---|---|---|---|---|
| 5 | 5 | 8 | 5 | 2 | 8 | 6 | 5 | 8 |

*For map, see p. 203.*

# THE RESORT

Westendorf is sometimes accused of being "instant Tyrol". And if that is the worst slur to be cast on this picturesque little settlement in the Kitzbühel Alps, the village fathers should be happy. The combination of Westendorf's pretty appearance combined with fresco-daubed, onion-domed church, nursery slopes starting at the village centre, the locals' sunny disposition and traditional après-ski, make it a perfect place to learn to ski. Best suited to complete beginners and improving second- or third-time skiers, Westendorf offers little challenge on the mountain, but plenty to do at night.

# THE SKIING

The Skigrossraum Wilder Kaiser-Brixental lift pass also covers Brixen, Hopfgarten, Söll, Ellmau, Itter and Going, meaning that better skiers can jump on the bus to a different place each morning.

But most of Westendorf's guests are content to take their first hesitant steps on the wide, almost flat, apron of nursery slopes by the church and, snowplough turns mastered, head up the Nachsöllberg (1886 m.) where the terrain is a little more exciting and the views such that you believe you really have achieved on-top-of-the-world status.

Although the skiing here is generally easy, as are most of the descents to the valley, Westendorf holds one or two surprises for the unwary, notably the steep and bumpy run directly between the summit and middle-station restaurant, which has a small terrace—much coveted on sunny days.

# APRÈS-SKI

Dinner jackets, even ties, are out of place, as nightlife is informal, lively and friendly, but at the same time civilized. The fun starts immediately after the day's exertions, instructors explaining that it is a skiing tradition for their charges to buy them a drink at the end of the day in one of the cafés, such as Gerry's Inn, at the bottom of the lift system.

With most of the hotels close by, the early-evening knees-up

doesn't preclude a good dinner, after which you have time to explore the various *Keller* and discos. Many hotels have live entertainment without cover charge, making bar-hopping easy. Alternatively, most tour operators offer the usual programme of fondues, disco night, tobogganing and the inevitable "Tyrolean evening" which involves drinking lots of beer and schnapps.

The highlight of the week for everyone in ski school is the prize-giving ceremony-cum-bunfight.

## OTHER ACTIVITIES

Two hotels have private swimming pools and fitness facilities, there is skating and curling early in the season, and tobogganing and bowling are available. There is extensive cross-country skiing, and accomplished skiers can venture as far as Kitzbühel; for the less ambitious, a 7-km. circuit starts at the village. Non-skiers have 10 km. of cleared paths for walking. Sleigh-rides to Annerhof are very popular.

# ZAUCHENSEE/ KLEINARL

Access: *Nearest airport:* Salzburg (45 mins.). *By road:* A10 motorway, exit Eben. *By rail:* to St.Johann im Pongau, then by bus.

Tourist Office: A-5602 Kleinarl. Tel. (06418) 206

| | |
|---|---|
| Altitude: 1014 m.(Kleinarl) *Top:* 1980 m. | Lifts: 36 (86 on Top-Tauern-Skischeck) |
| Language: German | Ski areas: Zauchensee, Kleinarl |
| Beds: 1,400 in Kleinarl | Ski schools: Schischule Zauchensee, Schischule Kleinarl |
| Population: 692 in Kleinarl | |
| Health: Doctor in resort. *Hospital:* Schwarzach (25 km.) | Linked resorts: Flachauwinkl |
| | Season: December to April |
| Runs: 80 km. | Kindergarten: *Non-ski:* none. *With ski:* 4–14 years. |

Prices: *Lift pass:* 6 days 880–1105 S (children 570–675 S). *Ski school:* Group 960 S for 6 days; private 380 S per hour.

# RATINGS

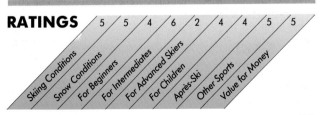

| Skiing Conditions | Snow Conditions | For Beginners | For Intermediates | For Advanced Skiers | For Children | Après-Ski | Other Sports | Value for Money |
|---|---|---|---|---|---|---|---|---|
| 5 | 5 | 4 | 6 | 2 | 4 | 4 | 5 | 5 |

*For map, see p. 35.*

# THE RESORT

Neither of these Salzburgerland villages is in the mainstream of sought-after resorts, but their combined skiing areas provide intermediates with endless opportunities for fast and furious attacks on the marked trails, with a few steep sections to test nerve and stamina en route. Each has good facilities for beginners, and for experts Zauchensee and Kleinarl are included on the Top-Tauern-Skischeck, which is valid in a score of resorts in Salzburgerland and Styria, making them excellent destinations for a couple of days when exploring this massive ski playground.

If any endorsement of the region's ability to provide top-quality skiing is needed, Kleinarl's most famous daughter is the incomparable Annemarie Moser-Pröll whose World Cup downhill exploits brought enormous pride to the whole of Austria and whose café, today, attracts her countrymen in droves, each of them delighted to be served a *Glühwein* or *Jägertee* by the great lady herself.

Zauchensee is just 5 km. up the valley from Altenmarkt and is little more than a small ski station with a handful of hotels. Kleinarl is much more of a village community featuring lots of hotels and *Gasthöfe*, as well as several disco-bars.

# THE SKIING

For a proficient skier, the full trek from Zauchensee to Kleinarl and back can be managed easily in a day, and there are several interesting diversions to make a week's stay varied and rewarding. A glance at the piste map reveals the necessity to cross the Salzburg-Villach *Autobahn*, yet this is the most charming interlude of the day: the Winkl Express storms its way under the *Autobahn*—well, it "storms" as well as a tractor disguised as a steam locomotive can! The upper sections of the slopes are quite exposed and the lower trails tree-lined and protected down to both villages.

# APRÈS-SKI

Zauchensee, with few overnight visitors, is understandably low-key, and even Altenmarkt down the valley fails to meet the needs of sophisticated socialites looking for glamorous après-ski, but it is a friendly village, ideal for anyone looking for a no-hype skiing holiday. Kleinarl is livelier and for those with their own transport—there are plenty more bars, discos and nightclubs down the road at Wagrain. Unpretentious eating, drinking and dancing are very much stock-in-trade in both places, and each offers traditional regional music evenings.

## OTHER ACTIVITIES

This region of the Tauern Alps has seemingly unlimited cross-country skiing trails, plus many cleared paths for walking. Although there is curling, tobogganing, table tennis and sleigh-rides, neither village provides the all-round sports facilities found in larger Austrian resorts. The better hotels, however, have swimming pool, Jacuzzi and sauna.

# ZELL AM SEE/ KAPRUN

Access: *Nearest airport:* Salzburg (1 hr.); Munich (2½ hrs.). *By road:* A8 motorway, exit Siegsdorf. *By rail:* railway station in Zell am See, bus to Kaprun.

Tourist Office: A-5710 Kaprun. Tel. (06547) 86 43

A-5700 Zell am See. Tel. (06542) 26 00

| | |
|---|---|
| Altitude: 750 m. (Zell am See) 800 m. (Kaprun) *Top:* 3029 m. | Ski areas: Maiskogel, Kitzsteinhorn, Schmittenhöhe, Zeller Berg, Sonnkogel |
| Language: German | Ski schools: Schischule Kaprun, Schischule Zell am See, Schischule Zell am See/Schüttdorf, Schischule Stöphasius |
| Beds: 4,500 in Kaprun, 9,081 in Zell am See | |
| Population: 2,800 (Kaprun), 8,700 (Zell am See) | |
| | Linked resorts: None |
| Health: Doctors in Zell am See and Kaprun. *Hospital:* Zell am See | Season: Beginning December to end April; summer skiing |
| Runs: 125 km. | Kindergarten: *Non-ski:* from 3 years. *With ski:* from 4 years. |
| Lifts: 51 | |

Prices: *Lift pass:* 6 days 1,180–1,400 S (children 765–910 S). *Ski school:* Group 340 S per day; private 380 S per hour.

# RATINGS

| Skiing Conditions | Snow Conditions | For Beginners | For Intermediates | For Advanced Skiers | For Children | Après-Ski | Other Sports | Value for Money |
|---|---|---|---|---|---|---|---|---|
| 7 | 8 | 5 | 8 | 4 | 5 | 6 | 7 | 6 |

# THE RESORTS

These two Salzburgerland towns style themselves, rather grandly, as the Europa Sport Region. In fact, each is an excellent resort with different features, and they share a lift pass which encompasses the full gamut of skiing. Zell am See is a bustling little town and a popular summer holiday destination, especially for watersports enthusiasts. Kaprun, a pretty, rambling village, is much quieter and in summertime attracts national teams and holidaymakers for skiing on the Kitzsteinhorn glacier.

There is a full range of hotels, from Zell am See's renovated Grand Hotel on the lakeside with adjacent health facilities) to Kaprun's Gasthof Mühle which specializes in wholesome regional dishes cooked and served in a large pan.

# THE SKIING

Zell am See, with two World Cup downhill courses and stunning views over the frozen lake below, and Kaprun, a year-round ski centre which has guaranteed snow every day of the year on the Kitzsteinhorn glacier, combine to provide long tree-lined pistes, wide, open bowls, narrow gullies and gentle nursery slopes.

The region's claim to providing guaranteed snow means that whilst it is comforting to know that there will be skiing of some sort in even the worst winters, this is offset by the danger that if conditions are poor in nearby low-lying centres, everyone will flock to Kaprun with resultant queues and overcrowding.

More positively, the two resorts provide just about the full range of on-piste skiing. The glacial slopes of Kaprun's upper area contrast with the excitement of taking Zell am See's tree-clad downhill trails at full tilt. Zell am See has three cable cars serving the crescent-shaped ridge above town, and if the downhill courses are thrilling, there is plenty of easy cruising, some diverting mogul fields and several long runs.

At Kaprun, there is a variety of lifts around the village, leading to some very pleasant easy slopes—low-lying, they can be closed in early and late season. For the Kitzsteinhorn, the Gletscherbahn funicular railway departs from outside the village and rises through the mountain to the Alpincenter from where drag lifts and chair lifts disperse skiers around the glacier.

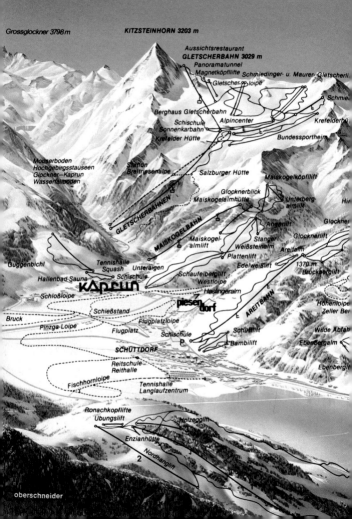

Grossglockner 3798 m

KITZSTEINHORN 3203 m

Aussichtsrestaurant
GLETSCHERBAHN 3029 m
Panoramatunnel
Magnetköpfllifte
Schmiedinger- u. Maurer- Gletscherli
Gletscher- loipe
Schmie...

Berghaus Gletscherbahn
Schischule
Alpincenter
Krefelderhü...
Sonnenkarbahn
Krefelder Hütte
Bundessportheim

Mooserboden
Hochgebirgsstauseen
Glockner–Kaprun
Wasserfallboden
Station Breitriesenalpe
Salzburger Hütte
Maiskogelköpfllift

GLETSCHERBAHNEN
Glocknerblick
Maiskogelalmhütte
Unterberg- almlift
Hi...

MAISKOGELBAHN
Angerlift
Glockner...

Maiskogel- almlift
Stanger
Weißsteinalm
Glocknerlift
Areitalm
1370 m
Bruckberglift

Tennishalle
Squash
Unteraigen
Plattenlift
Edelweißlift

Guggenbichl
Schaufelberglift
Westloipe

Hallenbad-Sauna
Schischule
KAPRUN
Haslingeralm

Schloßloipe
piesendorf

Schießstand
AREITBAHN
Höhenloipe
Zeller Ber...

Bruck
Flugplatzloipe
Schüttlift
Wilde Abfah...

Pinzga-Loipe
Flugplatz
Schischule
Bambilift
Ebenbergalm
Eberbergli...

SCHÜTTDORF

Reitschule
Reithalle
Ebenbergli...

Fischhornloipe
Tennishalle
Langlaufzentrum

Ronachkopflifte
Übungslift
Holzeggli...

Enzianhütte
2
Nordhanglift

oberschneider

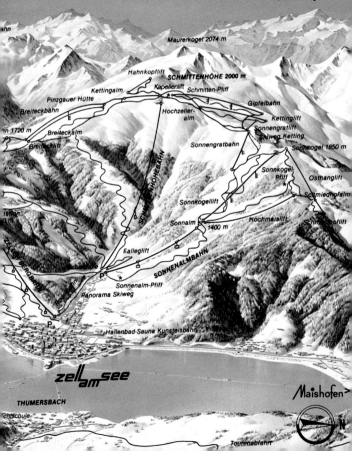

Grossvenediger 3674 m

Maurerkogel 2074 m

SCHMITTENHÖHE 2000 m

Hahnkopflift

Kettingalm        Kapellenlift    Schmitten-Pfiff

Pinzgauer Hütte                    Hochzeller-        Gipfelbahn
                                   alm
Breiteckbahn                                          Kettinglift
                                                      Sonnengratlift
Breiteckalm                        Sonnengratbahn     Skiweg Ketting
h 1720 m                                              Sonnkogel 1850 m
Breitecklift
                                   Sonnkogel-         Osthanglift
                                   Pfiff
                                                      Schmiedhofalm
                   Sonnkogellift

                   Sonnalm    1400 m    Hochmaislift
                                                      Schmittenhoflift
                   Falleglift
                              SONNENALMBAHN

                   Sonnenalm-Pfiff
            Panorama Skiweg

            P.
                   Hallenbad-Sauna Kunsteisbahn

zell am see

                                                      Maishofen

THUMERSBACH

chischule                                             N

Tourenabfahrt

There is a cable car to the region's highest point (3029 m.) where the open area below is ideal for perfecting technique or bombing furiously all day. In summer, it is a centre for national teams' training camps, as well as for recreational skiers who relish the prospect of skiing under a deep, deep blue sky. Kaprun's Kitzsteinhorn is also an excellent place for beginners to make their first runs in a clement climate—so different from tumbling down icy pistes in February.

# APRÈS-SKI

Kaprun is a dispersed village, without true *Gemütlichkeit*, but with a certain charm. Since it lacks a real centre, bar-hopping is difficult. The compensation is that it is friendly and, once inside, the night spots are merry and informal. Several restaurants feature the regional speciality of meat and vegetables cooked in a huge frying pan over an open fire. Zell am See is much more lively, and if at first sight it seems far removed from the old-fashioned ski *Dorf* of Austrian tourist propaganda, all the traditional pursuits such as tobogganing, sleigh-rides, drinking in *Weinstuben* to the accompaniment of zither and accordion, Tyrolean evenings and tea dances are all available. There is plenty of shopping, and some of the hotels have top-rate health facilities.

# OTHER ACTIVITIES

The Europa Sport Region has enormous possibilities for cross-country skiing: around Zell am See, the frozen lake is the constant focal point, and Kaprun hosts an annual marathon which is an integral part of the cross-country skiing calendar. Skating and walking on the lake are popular, and the leisure centre at Kaprun is especially well appointed. Ice hockey and skating contests are absorbing spectator sports. Indoor tennis, squash, rifle shooting and bowling are available, and when it is cold enough, there is curling.

The post bus service is efficient for exploring locally, and the railway makes visits to Kitzbühel, St. Johann in Tirol and St. Johann im Pongau (for skiing) and to Innsbruck and Salzburg (for a fix of city life) very easy.

# ZELL AM ZILLER

Access: *Nearest airport:* Munich (2 hrs.). *By road:* A12 motorway, exit Wiesing/Zillertal. *By rail:* to Jenbach, then by bus or Zillertalbahn.

Tourist Office: A-6280 Zell am Ziller. Tel. (05282) 22 81

Altitude: 580 m. *Top:* 2240 m.

Language: German

Beds: 5,200

Population: 1,800

Health: Doctors in resort. *Hospital:* Schwaz (40 km.)

Runs: 42 km.

Lifts: 24

Ski areas: Kreuzjoch, Gerlosstein

Ski schools: Schischule Lechner

Linked resorts: None

Season: Beginning December to mid-April

Kindergarten: *Non-ski:* from 4 years. *With ski:* from 4 years.

Prices: *Lift pass:* 6 days Zillertal 950–1,160 S (children 700 S). *Ski school:* Group 960 S for 5 days; private 320 S per hour.

## RATINGS

| Skiing Conditions | Snow Conditions | For Beginners | For Intermediates | For Advanced Skiers | For Children | Après-Ski | Other Sports | Value for Money |
|---|---|---|---|---|---|---|---|---|
| 6 | 5 | 7 | 6 | 3 | 6 | 6 | 6 | 7 |

# THE RESORT

After Mayrhofen, Zell is the Ziller valley's most popular destination for British skiers, most of them young and intent on having an energetic introduction to skiing and après-ski in equal proportions. The most common criticisms are that the skiing is a little way out of town and, being south-facing, has a comparatively short season. But it attracts a good number of repeat bookings because Zell is a friendly little town with sun-blessed slopes, an efficient ski bus system and, being the most central of the Zillertal resorts, is the ideal base for exploring the others, all available on the same lift pass.

With all this available, Zell am Ziller is an excellent choice for groups of mixed ability. Beginners confine themselves to the immediate vicinity, while intermediates and experts try a different place each day by driving or taking local buses or trains which are covered by lift passes valid for four days or more.

A low-key village, it falls at the mid-point between sophistication and rumbustiousness, and if you care to explore the string of tiny farming settlements along the eastern edge of the valley, there is the chance to experience unspoiled rustic Tyrolean life. The parish dates from A.D. 738 and in addition to farming, gold mining was a prosperous industry, as brewing continues to be—the brewery was founded in 1500 and is the oldest in the Tyrol.

# THE SKIING

Zell am Ziller's own territory is divided by the Gerlos valley. The Gerlosstein section is reached by either the cable car from Hainzenberg or a chair from Ramsau, each ten minutes away by the free bus service, and is tree-lined and mostly graded red with one black run beneath the Arbiskogel lift, plus an unpisted ski route back down to Ramsau.

The Kreuzjoch region, only a couple of minutes ride from the village centre, is served by a long gondola to the Wiesenalm (1309 m.) from where two chair lifts disperse skiers to either the Karspitze or the main Kreuzjoch runs—the two areas are connected higher up. The former has one of the easiest black runs imaginable—in major French centres it would barely be rated

219

red—but it is a thoroughly enjoyable run for good intermediates. The new Kreuzjoch lift has added a third black run, as well as some more sunny skiing.

There is a general tendency for runs to be graded too highly, possibly to give the generally lower-intermediate clientele a sense of achievement, yet it is a pleasant place to ski, with friendly restaurants and *Hütten* strategically placed at the end of trails. Families are particularly fortunate that the meeting places for both ski kindergarten and the day nursery are at altitude, making meeting for lunch easily arranged.

# APRÈS-SKI

There aren't many places buzzing with an excited chatter immediately after skiing other than the Café Reiter where tea dances are held, but the three discos do good trade later on and organized events such as fondue suppers and Tyrolean evenings at the Zellerhof are popular. An English-style "pub", the Piccadilly, caters to youngsters looking for an uncomplicated evening at uncomplicated prices.

# OTHER ACTIVITIES

Cross-country skiing is a speciality of the Zillertal, with a 24-km. *Loipe* to Mayrhofen (where there are lots more) as well as shorter ones close to hand; skating and curling take place, weather permitting, on a natural rink. The floodlit toboggan chute is reached by chair lift from Ramsau and runs down from the Sonnalm—nearly 5 km. long, it is a special feature of operators' programmes. The tourist office can suggest a variety of itineraries for walking on cleared paths, and two hotels have swimming pools and health facilities for residents. Nine-pin bowling takes place in the village and the ten-pin version in Hainzenberg.

If you have a car, take the old road on the eastern side of the valley, passing through Stumm and the twin hamlets of Bruck for a taste of old-fashioned Tyrolean life. Innsbruck is less than 40 minutes drive, and there are organized excursions to the regional capital, as well as to Salzburg and Italy's South Tyrol via the Brenner Pass.

# ZÜRS

Access: *Nearest airport:* Innsbruck (1½ hrs.); Zurich (2½ hrs.). *By road:* A14 to Bludenz, then over Flexenpass. *By rail:* to Langen, then by bus.

Tourist Office: A-6763 Zürs am Arlberg. Tel. (05583) 22 45

| | |
|---|---|
| Altitude: 1720 m. *Top:* 2850 m. | Lifts: 10 (74 in Arlberg) |
| Language: German | Ski areas: Trittkopf, Zürsersee, Muggengrat, Hexenboden |
| Beds: 1,350 | |
| Population: 130 | Ski schools: Schischule Zürs |
| Health: Doctor and fracture clinic in resort. *Hospital:* Bludenz (40 km.) | Linked resorts: Lech |
| | Season: End November to end April |
| Runs: 110 km. with Lech (300 km. on Arlberg pass) | Kindergarten: *Non-ski:* 3–10 years. *With ski:* 3–12 years. |

Prices: *Lift pass:* 6 days Arlberg Skipass 1,340–1,530 S (children 770–890 S). *Ski school:* Group 1,250 S for 6 days; private 1,650 S per day.

# RATINGS

| Skiing Conditions | Snow Conditions | For Beginners | For Intermediates | For Advanced Skiers | For Children | Après-Ski | Other Sports | Value for Money |
|---|---|---|---|---|---|---|---|---|
| 8 | 8 | 5 | 8 | 8 | 6 | 6 | 5 | 5 |

*For map, see pp. 154–155.*

# THE RESORT

Zürs is posh. Zürs attracts Europe's *glitterati*. Zürs is a bit precious. Zürs is also an excellent ski centre, 5 km. from Lech and within a short drive or bus ride of Stuben, St. Christoph and St. Anton, all of them included on the Arlberg lift pass.

To many, this tiny settlement is at the heart of the most interesting and demanding skiing area of the Alps and, like its neighbour, Lech, it is a choice spot for Europe's royalty and jet-set community. On approaching Zürs, the village looks like an ancient rustic community, but closer inspection reveals that although there are a few old buildings, most are modern hotels constructed in traditional chalet style, all of them beautifully

furnished and boasting opulent facilities. Most are appropriately expensive, and even the *Gasthöfe* are of the highest order.

With a limited number of guest beds, Zürs is assured of maintaining its exclusive status, but if you are staying in any of the neighbouring Arlberg centres, be sure to visit it for the excellent skiing and special atmosphere.

# THE SKIING

All skiing in the immediate vicinity is above the tree line and so, in the depths of winter, it is essential to dress warmly and avoid wind-ravaged chair lifts by using T-bars instead. Not that this is a problem for many visitors to Zürs as, even in more clement weather, the bars and restaurants are crowded with a beautifully dressed clientele more intent on cutting a dash than carving a turn. This is not to say that there isn't good skiing in Zürs—far from it. It is an excellent centre for fast on-piste skiing and, if full use is made of the Arlberg lift pass, there is a seemingly limitless range of opportunities for the best of skiers.

Off-piste, too, there is enormous scope. The circuit of trails linking Lech and Zürs provides a lot of testing work, and further afield, reached by car, taxi or the excellent post bus service, Stuben, St. Christoph and St. Anton combine to produce the full range of skiing experiences.

True experts, who must be accompanied by a guide, relish the off-piste return from the Valluga peak above St. Anton back to Zürs. For a more expensive thrill, there is a helicopter station outside Zürs along the Flexenpass and another just outside St. Anton for getting-away-from-it-all powder skiing in otherwise inaccessible bowls and gullies. The only possible criticism is that, being well above the tree line, there is little shelter should the weather close in.

# APRÈS-SKI

Zürs has a very high proportion of visitors who return year after year, engendering the atmosphere of an exclusive club. The bars and nightclubs are sophisticated but certainly not stuffy, and several of the grander hotels have live bands each evening, as well as smaller places for a drink and romantic chat.

# OTHER ACTIVITIES

Dressing up, in the most opulent ski and après-ski wear, is probably the most popular pastime other than skiing—rivalled only by going shopping in Lech.

For those with a romantic turn of mind, moonlit sleigh-rides are offered, and cross-country skiers have 4 km. of trails in Zürs with 13 km. more in neighbouring Lech. Otherwise, facilities in hotels include swimming, sauna, table-tennis, billiards, gym, bowling, indoor golf and tennis.

# BERLITZ SKI-INFO

An A-Z Summary of Practical Information, Facts and Advice

## CONTENTS

# A ACCOMMODATION

**Hotels.** Accommodation ranges from small, family hotels, through the large but basic variety, up to expensive luxury. You usually get what you pay for, but there is also a one- to five-star rating to guide you. The better hotels usually have saunas, Jacuzzi, swimming pool and massage facilities. Austria's few custom-built resorts feature several-storey, modern hotels with small bedrooms and large dining areas, while traditional villages offer a wider choice. Almost all hotels have comfortable bars.

**Gasthöfe** are small hotels/guest houses generally run by a resident family and are invariably spotless.

**Chalets.** A catered chalet holiday is a very popular alternative to hotel accommodation. A tour operator normally takes over a chalet-style residence and provides it with English-speaking staff. You can choose from a cosy six-some to a jumbo chalet, which is more like a hotel, often with its own bar and discotheque. Chalets can sometimes be taken on a self-catering basis.

**Apartments.** These, like chalets, can be anything from a small studio to luxury accommodation with en suite bathrooms and south-facing balconies. If all you want to do is ski hard all day and crash out at night after dining in a local restaurant, a tiny studio is fine. It's easiest to book through a tour company and claim a reduction if not using the flight or through private owners (also good for self-catering chalets) via small ads in skiing magazines. Lists of addresses and telephone numbers are also available through the Austrian National Tourist Office in London (see under TOURIST INFORMATION OFFICE).

**Caravans.** Some ski resorts have caravan sites, but for out-in-the-elements accommodation such as this, your caravan or camper bus would need to be specially fitted with boosted heating facilities. The discomfort would be offset by the possibility of resort-hopping on a regular basis if so desired.

## AIRPORTS                                                                    A

There are three Austrian airports within easy reach of most skiing areas—Innsbruck, Klagenfurt and Salzburg. Munich is often used for reaching the Tyrol, while Zurich serves the Vorarlberg and Arlberg regions.

Innsbruck, due to the requirements of inch-perfect descent through the spectacular mountains surrounding the city, is used only by small passenger aircraft.

Salzburg is becoming increasingly popular among charter-flight operators, due to expansion, improved facilities and close proximity to resorts in Salzburgerland, Styria and eastern Tyrol.

Salzburg and Innsbruck are both served by mainline railway stations and each gives easy access to Kirchberg, Kitzbühel, St. Johann in Tirol, Zell am See and St. Johann im Pongau, plus a dozen smaller centres en route. They are also close to a motorway, making transfers by road very quick.

## BOOKING (See also INSURANCE.)                                               B

The market leaders in the ski tour operator business are best booked through a travel agent; some smaller companies will sell direct to the client.

If you are booking through a tour operator, air transport and transfer by coach to your resort are included in the cost of your holiday. Some will even offer you free or discounted travel from your home to the departure airport, especially if there is a group booking. These companies get very good flight deals, so if you make your own way but take their accommodation, you won't find you've made much of a saving. Some operators offer a coach alternative—cheaper, but also long and tiring.

Wading through tour operator brochures can sometimes be more confusing than helpful, until you know exactly what to look for, though even the most experienced sometimes find they haven't got what they want. Books exist solely on the subject of finding the right holiday to suit your needs and budget. Another idea is to look through the specialist magazines, especially around September and October, as they usually carry out detailed analyses of what's on offer.

**B**    Package tours cater for everyone—from all-inclusive learn-to-ski weeks (travel, accommodation, lift pass, equipment hire, tuition) to advanced off-piste powder weeks. Book with one of the giants for competitive prices in hotels or self-catering. Go through a specialist company for something different and personal service.

Many companies offer early-booking and full-payment discounts (brochures come out already in summer) and most 1 free place for every 10 bookings and discounts for children. Most companies now offer a snow guarantee whereby they transport you free of charge to a nearby resort with snow or refund you for every ski day lost. Read the small print at the end of the brochure and make sure you will get a full refund should the company cancel your trip, as well as fair refund if you have to back out; percentage refunds decrease the closer cancellation is to departure date. The tendency is for larger operators to give a better deal than the smaller ones.

Other interesting features in the brochures are special January reductions and free airport car parking. A few companies cater for long weekends and 10/11 night options and others offer gourmet chalet or luxury hotel accommodation.

You can, of course, arrange your holiday independently, but it works out cheaper in the long run to travel package.

## C CHILDREN

More and more parents are taking even tiny babies on skiing holidays. The modern idea is that the sooner the child is introduced to the snow environment the better, it being allowed to "grow up" on skis.

Several tour companies have recognized this market potential and provide English nannies. Many others have special family chalets, nanny weeks and crêche facilities. There is a great range of different reductions for children, so look out for good deals—even free places.

Even if you don't take a special package, if you select the right resort you can still find freedom. Make sure the local kindergarten caters for youngsters in the right age group (many only take two upwards). Older children can go to ski kindergarten where they will play in the snow and start learning to ski. From six upwards children are accepted at ski school proper. Don't worry about language difficulties, Austrian instructors are renowned for their good English. Some ski schools take the children all day and supervise lunch, others finish at midday.

Almost every resort offers ice skating and tobogganning as an alternative to skiing and some (especially those in the Vorarlberg province) organize special children's parties and fun skiing races. Look out for hotels billing themselves as "Baby Hotels". They offer special facilities for the very young.

Obviously children, particularly babies, will feel the cold, so do take adequate clothing. All-in-one padded suits are best, with a vest and a couple of lightweight jumpers underneath, mittens (attached to the suit or they'll disappear) and always a hat (preferably tied on) and a hood, which insulates the ears well. Sensitive eyes and skin must be well protected. Ordinary sunglasses will not do. Invest in a pair with 100 per cent UV (ultra-violet) and IR (infra-red) block. Use extra high protection sun block (Factor 15). Cold air dries babies' skin; your local chemist will be able to recommend a suitable cream to prevent this.

There is no need to take special supplies of baby foods, medicines or toiletries with you. Austrian chemists and supermarkets sell a fully comprehensive range of these items.

## CLIMATE

The climate in the Alps is extremely changeable. The higher the resort the colder it will be, but the sun will be strong when it's out. North-facing slopes will be colder than south-facing ones because they don't get the sun, but they will keep the snow longer. Take into account the wind-chill factor, especially if skiing at speed.

Recent Decembers have been warm and sunny, but disappointing with regard to snow cover. Watch out for frostbite in January and February (see HEALTH AND MEDICAL CARE), especially at the top of the mountain; it can be pleasant at resort level and a raging blizzard on high. March and April

**C** can be gloriously hot and sunny. Good snow lasts into April at higher resorts. Lower ones tend to get patchy in late March, south-facing slopes become slushy by midday and it has been known to rain! When it rains in the resort, it's snowing higher up the mountain, so all is not lost.

While skiing, you are often in the clouds. If it is foggy in the village, don't despair. You may well climb way above it to sunny slopes and look down on a sea of mist. Conversely, sometimes it's better to stick to lower slopes because the peak is in cloud.

The snow never melts in high glacial mountain areas. Summer weather can be equally deceptive. A sunny shirts-off day can deteriorate rapidly into arctic conditions. Remember it is much colder on the glacier than in the village below.

The resort tourist office usually pins the weather forecast outside for skiers to consult.

Snow reports and weather forecasts can be obtained by phone, but bulletins are in German:

| | |
|---|---|
| For lower Austria, Styria | (222) 1583 |
| For Salzburg, Upper Austria, Carinthia | (222) 1584 |
| For Tyrol, Vorarlberg | (222) 1585 |
| Weather in general | (222) 1566 |

## CLOTHING AND ACCESSORIES

Be prepared! Due to the vagaries of mountain weather (see CLIMATE) always err on the cautious side. It's better to sweat a bit than die of hypothermia. The outer ski suit can be a one-piece or ski pants (stretchy racing ones or padded salopettes) and a jacket. The advantage of the former is that snow can't get up your back and it's comfortable to wear. Choose a two-piece if you want the jacket to double as après-ski wear or even casual gear back home. The jacket will ideally have a high collar, incorporating a roll-up hood, and close-fitting cuffs. Look closely at the label: Gore-Tex, Entrant and Cyclone are waterproof; Thinsulate and Isodry supply lightweight warmth; Tactel is ICI's great, new waterproof fibre ideal for ski wear.

Several thin layers under your suit provide better insulation than a bulky jersey. Natural fibres—silk, cotton, wool—wick moisture away from the skin. A long-sleeved thermal vest and long johns are essential, with a cotton skiing roll-neck and possibly another thin woollen jumper or a sweatshirt. It really depends on the thermal qualities of your suit, the weather and individual needs. If too hot, you can always take a layer off and tie it round your waist. It helps to carry a rucksack or bumbag to house accessories. You only need to wear one pair of tube-type ski socks (not ribbed).

Mitts are warmer than gloves, but you have to take them off to adjust boots and bindings. Either get leather handwear or Gore-Tex. Carry a pair of silk glove-liners and a silk balaclava just in case—frostbite sets in very quickly. A large percentage of body heat is lost through the head, so have a hat with you always. Headbands are good, too, for keeping the ears cosy.

Goggles and specs are most important. Always take both with you whatever the weather in the valley. A yellow-amber tint gives best definition. Altitude and reflection off the snow increase damage to the cornea caused by ultra-violet radiation. Make sure the lenses block out UV, and infra-red if possible. Darker lenses are more dangerous because the pupil dilates, allowing more rays in.

Although ski wear has become a fashion commodity, practicality should take precedence over colour and style.

**Après-ski.** Take loose and comfortable clothes to change into for the evening after the rigours of a day's labours on the slopes. Few hotels observe formal dining requirements, but it's a good idea for men to take a tie in case circumstances demand. Dancing in après-ski boots is difficult, so if you visit a local discotheque, it's not a bad idea to have a pair of lightweight shoes or slippers tucked into your pocket or bag.

# DRIVING

To take your car into Austria you will need:

- International Driving Permit or, for Europeans, a national driving licence

**D** • Car registration papers
• Third party insurance (the Green Card is not obligatory, but comprehensive coverage is always advisable).
• Nationality plate or sticker
• Red warning triangle
• First-aid kit

In order not to dazzle oncoming traffic at night, you can buy special black tape to mask a portion of the left-hand side of the headlights. These stickers come in sizes to suit your car model and are obtainable from local dealers.

Naturally, you should ensure that your car is in excellent working order and likely to stand up to the extreme conditions encountered in mountain driving (and parking). If your car engine is water cooled, make sure you have a good anti-freeze, and a strong solution for the windscreen wash. A tow rope and shovel are recommended.

**Driving regulations.** As elsewhere on the continent, drive on the right, overtake on the left. Be sure to observe the following:

• Seat belts are obligatory.
• Children under 12 may not sit in the front.
• On the motorway *(Autobahn),* passing another vehicle on the right is prohibited.
• Vehicles coming from the right have priority at crossroads without other signals.
• Trams have priority, even when coming from the left.
• Vehicles must halt behind trams when they are slowing to a halt, embarking or disembarking passengers.
• It is prohibited to use the horn (day or night) in town.
• Motorcyclists must wear crash helmets and use dipped headlights throughout the day.

Drunken driving is a very serious offence in Austria. The permissible alcohol level in the blood is 0.8 per mille.

**Speed limits.** On motorways 130 kph (around 80 mph) or 100 kph (around 60 mph); on other roads 100 kph or 80 kph (50 mph); in built-up areas 50 kph (31 mph).

**Motoring organizations.** There are two motoring orga- **D**
nizations in Austria: Österreichischer Automobil-, Motorrad-
und Touring-Club (ÖAMTC), Schubertring 1–3, 1010 Vienna,
tel. (222) 7299-0; and the Auto-, Motor- und Radfahrerbund
Österreichs (ARBÖ), Mariahilferstrasse 180, 1150 Vienna, tel.
(222) 85 35 35.

In Britain, consult the Automobile Association (AA), Fanum
House, Basingstoke, Hants, tel: (0256) 20123; or the Royal
Automobile Club (RAC), P.O. Box 100, RAC House, Lans-
downe Road, Croydon, Surrey, tel: (01) 686 2525.

The AA and RAC both produce excellent booklets, *Guide
to Motoring Abroad* and *Continental Motoring Guide*. The
latter also has a section on toll roads and mountain passes.
Both also have special insurance schemes for members and
non-members, and the AA can furnish you with a Green
Card.

**Road conditions.** Certain motorways and tunnels charge
tolls, notably the Brenner, Gleinalmtunnel, Felbertauern and
Tauern motorways, the Grossglockner Alpine road and the
Arlberg Tunnel.
Road and traffic conditions (ÖAMTC): (222) 1590

**Breakdowns.** Austrian automobile clubs offer 24-hour
breakdown services to all drivers on motorways and main
roads.

|  |  |
|---|---|
| ÖAMTC | 120 |
| ARBÖ | 123 |

In the event of a breakdown, switch on your flashing warning
lights and place your red warning triangle 50 m. behind your
car (and not more than 1 m. from the kerb). It's wise to take
out internationally valid breakdown insurance before leav-
ing home and to ask for an estimate before repairs are
undertaken.

**Mountain roads.** Gradients of between 6 and 15 per cent are
common in the Alps. Caravans and trailers are banned on
certain routes. Vehicles must be equipped with snow tyres,
spikes or chains in snow conditions. A bus or lorry going
uphill has priority.

**D** There is a special art to driving on ice and in snowy conditions. The golden rule is always to drive more slowly than you think you should. Avoid sharp reactions or sudden braking; it's better to anticipate well in advance, such as keeping a good distance from the car in front (two or three times the normal braking distance). When starting off or going uphill, put the car in the highest possible gear to avoid wheel spin. Never drive in ski or après-ski boots.

**Parking.** Some resorts do not allow cars to circulate and, although you can drop luggage off, you have to leave the car in a special parking area. To use most town-centre car parks (*Kurzparkzone*), you need a parking voucher (*Parkscheine*), which must be clearly displayed on the inside of the windscreen, showing both arrival and departure times, and valid from between ½ hour and 1 ½ hours. You can buy these from tobacco kiosks or post offices.

Try to park your car in a place where it, or at least the engine, is sheltered from the wind, and the handbrake can be left off to avoid it being frozen on. But then don't forget to leave the car in gear! Pull windscreen wipers away from the glass.

**Roofracks.** Skiing luggage, if you have all the equipment, can be excessive. Boxes which fit onto the roof are excellent (though expensive) and protect skis and other belongings from the elements. Regular ski roofracks cost less and can also be hired from some ski hire shops or the AA.

**Winter tyres and snow chains.** You can get your car fitted with winter tyres which grip better than regular tyres, but even these may not be good enough for some snowy mountain roads. Studded tyres are subject to restrictions: there is a speed limit of 80 kph outside built-up areas and of 100 kph on motorways; they can only be used from around mid-November to mid-April (dates vary from year to year); and only on vehicles with steel radial tyres and weighing less than 3,500 kg.

On many mountain roads it is obligatory to have chains in the car even if conditions do not necessitate their use. They come in various tyre sizes and vary in price usually

according to sophistication and ease of handling. They can
be rented from the ÖAMTC and the ARBÖ, major ski shops in
Britain and the AA (Dover branch only). **D**

Practise putting on your chains *before* you get stuck in
heavy snow.


## ENTRY REQUIREMENTS                                       **E**

British nationals need only a valid passport, either a full
British Passport, valid 10 years, or a British Visitor's Passport,
valid one year for trips to Austria.

United States, Australia, New Zealand and Canada nationals are admitted on production of a valid passport.

Here are some items you can take into Austria and into
your home country on your return.

| Into: | Cigarettes | Cigars | Tobacco | Spirits | Wine |
|---|---|---|---|---|---|
| Austria 1) | 200 or | 50 or | 250 g. | 1 l. and | 2 l. |
| 2) | 400 or | 100 or | 500 g. | 1 l. and | 2 l. |
| Australia | 200 or | 250 g. or | 250 g. | 1 l. or | 1 l. |
| Canada | 200 and | 50 and | 250 g. | 1.1 l. or | 1.1 l. |
| Eire | 200 or | 50 or | 250 g. | 1 l. and | 2 l. |
| N. Zealand | 200 or | 50 or | 250 g. | 1.1 l. or | 4.5 l. |
| S. Africa | 400 and | 50 and | 250 g. | 1 l. and | 2 l. |
| U.K. | 200 or | 50 or | 250 g. | 1 l. and | 2 l. |
| U.S.A. | 200 and | 100 and | 3) | 1 l. or | 1 l. |

1) Arriving from European countries.
2) Arriving from non-European countries.
3) A reasonable quantity.


**EQUIPMENT** (See also CLOTHING AND ACCESSORIES.)

First of all you need to decide whether to buy or hire and
then whether to do so at home or in the resort. If you're a
beginner there is no point in buying skis and boots. Once
you have the bug and have reached intermediate standard,
you might consider getting your own gear.

**E**   If you hire in Britain, you'll get the chance to try the boots on a dry slope (or at least wear them round the house), and if they hurt or are loose, change them. On the other hand you will be burdened with extra baggage. You can hire from Airport Skis (Gatwick and Manchester) who will reimburse you if the boots don't fit and you have to re-hire in the resort.

Hiring in the resort could waste a lot of time. Everyone rushes to the hire shop on the first morning, the staff may be overworked, communication might be tricky and you could be ill-fitted. If not totally satisfied with your equipment, take it back and change it. Painful boots and unsuitable skis can ruin a holiday.

Boots should fit snugly and the heel should not lift up when you're leaning forward. Don't make the mistake of doing them up too tightly (it will cut the circulation and be very painful), nor pad out boots that are too big with several layers of socks. Rear-entry boots are easiest to deal with for a beginner. Classic clip boots give more control to expert skiers.

Your forearm should be parallel with flat ground when holding the pole. To test this, turn the pole upside down and grip it below the basket. You can either choose a pole with a sword grip (easy to use) or strap (less likely to get lost in a fall). Most poles have a combination of both.

Opinions on the right length of ski follow fashion trends. Much depends on the type of ski (e.g. recreational, special, competition), and the weight and ability of the skier. If you get a ski which is either too long or too stiff it will spoil your skiing. Beginners should go for flexible, relatively short skis for easy turning. Stiff, long skis require precision technique, but will hold icy slopes better. Flexible skis, however, perform best in powder snow.

Buyers and hirers alike should ensure that the shop technician has regulated the binding (DIN) setting to suit the weight and ability of the skier.

Finally, look after your skis. Get them hot-waxed every two days (even hire skis) for optimum performance. Keep the edges sharp to maintain control on hardpacked snow. Save money by learning how to do it yourself.

**GETTING THERE** (See also BOOKING.)          **G**

## Air

If booking independently you need to decide whether to travel by scheduled or charter flight. Tour operators often offer charter-flight seats at lower fares than those on scheduled services. However, scheduled services are also discounted through flight sales agencies close to the date of departure. These agencies advertise in national newspapers and are often good for last-minute bargains. Normally, though, there is a bewildering array of tickets for scheduled services, with prices for the same class of seating varying greatly depending on when you book and how long you want to stay.

If you are travelling on a tour operator's charter flight, there may well be space on their connecting coach, so buying a seat right through to the resort will save you trouble.

## Coach

There are no independent coach services to Austria. Some tour operators offer coach as an alternative to flying— cheaper, but also long and tiring.

## Rail

This is a good choice if travelling independently, especially if going to a resort either with, or close to, a railway station, as it can cut transfer times considerably. You can also take a night train, book a sleeper, have a nice dinner and wake up in the Alps. On arrival, there are buses which meet the train and transport you to the resort. The Arlberg Express will convey you direct from the Channel coast to Innsbruck, Salzburg or St. Anton. This is normally a daily service. In other cases, a change is required en route.

For local train times and prices contact Austrian Federal Railways *(Österreichische Bundesbahnen—ÖBB),* at the Austrian National Tourist Office (see under TOURIST INFORMATION OFFICE). Information can also be obtained from the European Rail Travel Centres at major railway stations in most British cities. They can help with prices, timings and booking.

If travelling with skis, you are advised to register these three or four days before departure at the Registered

239

**G** Baggage Office at Victoria Station. You will need to take your ticket along with you.

### Cross-Channel Ferry

There are plenty of Channel crossings each day. Remember sea conditions tend to be rougher in winter. A trip by Hovercraft is quicker and only slightly more expensive, but crossings are occasionally cancelled due to high seas. Some ferry lines offer special ski-package rates. Pick up a *Travel Agency Car Ferry Guide* for up-to-date details.

## H HEALTH AND MEDICAL CARE

Austria has a reciprocal health agreement with the British National Health Service, but this is not recognized by all doctors and hospitals and you are well advised to take out health insurance.

Even minor skiing injuries can turn out to be very expensive to treat, and a major accident could ruin you if your medical insurance were not adequate (see INSURANCE).

Make sure you get official receipts for everything: rescue service, doctor's or hospital fees, chemist prescriptions. Put in a claim as soon as you get home. There's usually a deadline.

Medical attention is not, of course, limited to traumatic skiing injuries. A nasty cold, flu or stomach upset may necessitate a visit to the doctor, although the local chemist (often displaying a red cross symbol) may be able to suggest a suitable remedy.

Mountain weather is deceptive (see CLIMATE), and not taking the correct precautions or being adequately dressed (see CLOTHING AND ACCESSORIES) can have serious repercussions. Here are a few of the dangers, and what to do if the worst happens.

**Altitude sickness.** Altitude alone affects many people. Mild altitude sickness experienced at around 3,000 m. includes severe headache, nausea and dizziness, but symptoms retreat within an hour of returning to base (your family doctor can prescribe a medicament to prevent this).

**Sunburn.** Even on a cloudy day you can burn. Put plenty of
high protection cream (Factor 15) on exposed areas concentrating on nose, lips, ears. Apply half an hour before going out to enable the skin to absorb it and reapply often.

**Snowblindness** occurs when the eyes are not adequately protected. The thin air at high altitude and reflection of the sun off the snow damages the eyes. The result can be most uncomfortable, somewhat like having grit or sand under the eyelids. Stay in a darkened room and bathe the eyes with a special lotion. Normal sight will return, but the cornea may suffer permanent damage.

**Frostbite** is when body tissue actually freezes. First signs are white patches on the face (especially nose and ears) and extremities and a total loss of sensation, even of cold. Usually, if the frostbite is on an exposed part of the body, it is a companion who first notices. If it is not too far advanced, a warm hand over the affected area or rewarming numb and icy fingers under the armpits will be sufficient to bring back sensation. *Never* rub a frostbitten part with snow. More advanced frostbite leads to blistering, and the area turns a greyish-blue colour. These are very serious symptoms and immediate expert medical treatment should be sought.

**Hypothermia** is the dangerous lowering of the body temperature. Symptoms are somnolence, apathy and lack of coordination, gradually leading to loss of consciousness. It is particularly common in avalanche victims, but can also be the result of insufficient nourishment, combined with extreme cold, high winds or wet. Again, it is the quick reaction of a companion that can avert more dangerous consequences. Get the victim warm, by putting on extra clothing or a covering—a hat, windjackets, sleeping bags or space blankets—that shield from the wind and conserve body heat. Huddling together or sharing body warmth can also be effective. If the victim is fully conscious, administer warm drinks. *Don't* give alcohol, it accelerates the loss of body heat; and *don't* encourage the victim to "move around to get warm".

**H Injury on the mountain.** Place crossed skis about 15 m. above the victim and ensure that he is as warm and as comfortable as possible. If it is a leg injury, do not remove ski boots, they act as a splint. Send a good skier to the nearest lift station: the attendant will radio the piste patrol, who are qualified to assess and deal with the injuries and transport the victim to the doctors or ambulance. They will also decide whether a helicopter rescue is necessary. Keep in mind that the piste patrol is not necessarily responsible for the safety and rescue of off-piste skiers (see SNOW CONDITIONS).

The international distress signal in the mountains is six shouts or whistles a minute followed by a minute's silence. Three calls or whistles a minute with a minute's silence is the reply.

## HOLIDAYS

The Austrians flock to the mountains and the pistes get overcrowded over Christmas, New Year and Easter. The Austrian equivalent of half-term varies from region to region, but all take place during the first two weeks of February. It's worth checking with the local tourist office that you are not planning your trip during the school holidays.

**I INSURANCE** (See also BOOKING and HEALTH AND MEDICAL CARE.)

Many tour operators insist that you take their insurance (partly to ensure you are adequately covered), so check it out well and if necessary take out additional coverage independently. Never economize on insurance.

Ideally your travel insurance will cover you for the following eventualities:

- cancellation or curtailment
- loss or theft of baggage en route, belongings in the resort
- loss or theft of personal money
- breakage of equipment
- illness
- accident on or off the slopes
- rescue service
- transport home

- third party or personal liability, i.e., damage done by you to someone else or their property.

Useful benefits not covered by all policies:

- missed departure, due to car accident or breakdown, or failure of public transport to deliver you to your departure airport on time (provided you have left sufficient time)
- facility for a friend or relative to stay on in the resort with you if you can't travel immediately or, if necessary, travel with you on a different flight from the rest of the package tour group
- loss of earnings due to the effects of an injury resulting from your ski accident
- refund on lift pass for every ski day lost through injury

Look closely at the exclusion clauses which state the circumstances in which an insurance company won't settle a claim. On each claim, there is usually an "excess", which is the difference between what the insurance company will pay out and the amount the claimant actually lost or paid. The amount varies from policy to policy.


## LIFTS                                                                    L

New and more efficient lift systems are being introduced all the time, as more and more skiers want to get up the mountain faster than ever. The basic types are:

**Drag or tow lifts.** These pull you up the mountain on your skis. One type consists of a saucer-sized disc or "button" which you slip between your legs and place behind your bottom. First-timers should remember *not* to sit down, to keep their skis parallel and to relax as much as possible. If you sit down, the elastic wire attached to the disk will give under your weight and you will fall over. Your first time on a drag lift could be an unnerving experience, but most lift operators are sympathetic and will slow the lift down and help you on if you manage to communicate your fears to them. Button tows are less common in Austria than in other countries.

**L**    It is fair to say that T-bars, which pull up two people at a time, are universally unpopular. It helps to pick a partner the same size. Tips for riding them well include leaning inwards and keeping the outer ski slightly forwards.

**Chair lifts** have improved in leaps and bounds over the years, going from single chairs right up to four-seater express lifts which slow down to let you on, then accelerate off at breakneck speed. Advantages: you don't need to take off your skis, so they are quick and easy, and it's pleasant to sit and relax on a sunny day. They are also a good way down from the higher slopes if the low ones are balding or difficult to ski for other reasons. Disadvantages: it can be freezing on a chair lift (some have built-in covers to wrap around you as you ascend); if it's windy they close them down, but on the odd occasion when you're going up on one just before the wind is considered too strong to operate it, the ride can be most uncomfortable; they have a habit of stopping and bouncing mid-route.

**Gondolas** *(Gondelbahn)*. Often called "eggs" or "bubbles", these are little cabins (which vary from four- to new eight-seater express) in which you sit, placing skis in a rack outside. They take you way up the mountain in some comfort and you are protected from the elements.

**Cable cars** *(Seilbahn)* have reached mammoth proportions over the years. You stand in them, holding your skis. Some can carry over 150 skiers at a time. Every new one installed takes a few extra skiers, so the resort can boast the biggest cable car, for a while.
   A new lift system pioneered in the last couple of seasons combines the *Gondelbahn* with the *Seilbahn*. This consists of a string of carriages on a cable (like the *Gondelbahn*), but instead of a few skiers sitting, more than 20 skiers can stand in each. It's a very fast way of getting a large number of skiers up the mountain.

**Lift passes.** Choosing the right type of lift ticket to suit your needs can be difficult. If you are a beginner, there is no need to get a pass for the whole area. Many resorts do not charge

for the nursery lifts. A good system for beginners is the **L**
punch card. You purchase a card with so many points and
each lift is worth a certain number which the operator
punches off the card. More advanced skiers can either buy a
daily lift pass, which is best if you don't plan to ski every day.
You save money, however, if you get a block pass—six days
for a week's holiday—but you'll need to have a passport-size
photo with you. For the vast interlinked ski areas, you then
have the option of a pass covering part of the area or the
entire network. The choice really depends on your standard
and the size of the area involved: in some cases it is so vast,
an average intermediate would be hard-pressed to cover it
in a week. You can always get your local pass and pay a daily
supplement to ski in another part of the complex.

Don't forget to ask for a piste map of the area at the lift
ticket office. Easy runs are marked blue, red runs are more
tricky, and black runs are for expert skiers. Icy conditions,
slushy, melting snow, fog or a blizzard naturally make the
runs more difficult to ski.

## MONEY MATTERS **M**

**Currency.** Austria's monetary unit is the *Schilling*, abbreviat-
ed S, ÖS or Sch. It is divided into 100 *Groschen*. There are
coins of 10 and 50 Groschen and 1, 5, 10 and 20 Schillings.
Banknotes are found in denominations of 20, 50, 100, 500 and
1,000 Schillings. The 10 and 50 Groschen coins look very
similar to the 5 and 10 Schilling pieces, and the new 100 and
1,000 Schilling notes can also easily be confused, so always
check carefully.

**Credit cards and traveller's cheques.** Most major hotels and
many restaurants accept credit cards. Traveller's cheques
are welcome almost anywhere. Eurocheques are also widely
used.

**Banks and currency exchange.** Foreign currency can be
changed in banks and currency-exchange offices. Travel
agencies and hotels also change money, but the rate may not
be as good as at the bank.

# P PRICES

Prices in Austrian resorts vary a great deal depending on the smartness of the resort. In general, the higher you go, the more you pay. Some supermarket prices match those in Britain. Wines and local beers are cheaper, and cheeses and cold meats are good buys if self-catering and, if eating out, there are many excellent small family-run establishments which are well worth searching out.

In the resorts, bar and restaurant prices are similar to those found in London, and, by law, the tariff must be displayed outside, so a bit of "window-shopping" will soon determine the best value and the likely bill. Hearty soups and pastries are usually good value. Nightlife is cheaper than France or Switzerland. If a club charges an entrance fee, check whether this includes the price of a first drink. Otherwise, be prepared to pay some extraordinary prices.

The following prices will give you a rough idea of what to expect. Due to variations from resort to resort, and ever-present inflation, they should only be regarded as approximate:

**Airport transfer.** Salzburg–Kitzbühel (by rail) 184 S; Innsbruck–St. Anton (by rail) 142 S.

**Entertainment.** Cinema 45–60 S, admission to discotheque (incl. drink) 80–120 S, casino admission 100 S, cabaret (including drink) 300–600 S.

**Equipment hire** (skis, sticks and boots). 65–200 S.

**Cigarettes** (per packet of 20) 25–30 S.

**Hotels** (double room). ***** 1,500–3,000 S, **** 1,150–2,400 S, *** 500–1,000 S, **/* 300–350 S.

**Kindergarten.** Six days care and lunch 600–800 S.

**Meals and drinks.** Continental breakfast 80–100 S; mountain lunch 60–100 S, set menu 80–150 S, lunch/dinner in fairly good establishment 250–350 S, coffee 25 S, whisky or cocktail 50–100 S, beer/soft drink 20–25 S, cognac 50 S, bottle of wine from 100 S.

SKI SCHOOLS                                                    **S**

Austria, quite rightly, prides itself on its high standard of
tuition, and if any credentials are needed, it seems that every
ski school is headed by an Olympic, world or, at the least,
national champion. Since Hannes Schneider started giving
lessons in 1907 at St. Anton, Austria has defined techniques
and, the claims of the *ski évolutif* philosophy in France
notwithstanding, remains the most emulated method of
teaching—its "feet-together" style regarded as the classic
way to ski. Instructors are required to undergo a thoroughly
exhaustive regime of practice which includes teaching in
foreign languages, notably English.

Most resorts have a ski kindergarten, which caters for
children from five years, and classes are invariably fun.
Adult classes are similarly high-spirited, and whilst infinite
care in teaching skills is the main priority, it is usual for the
instructor to take his class for a beer or schnapps at the end of
the day—he doesn't expect to pay, however! A week's
course culminates in a race, with pins, medals or certificates
to be won, followed by dancing and much merry-making.

Safety is a high priority, as anyone who has incurred the
wrath of their ski *Lehrer* for careering away out of control
will testify. Good skiers should be encouraged to join ski
school, as the top class is usually competition-standard, its
participants intent on honing their technique to the highest
level through an intensive course of touring, powder skiing,
mogul work and slalom racing. Another reason for good
skiers to join a class is that it affords the opportunity of
experiencing top-quality guiding of the region's skiing
terrain with instruction thrown in. Be sure to consult your
instructor if you feel that you should move up, or down, a
grade. If you consider that personal tuition would iron out
some deficiencies, either ask him to give you (paid) extra
instruction at lunchtime or book a half-day lesson.

**SNOW CONDITIONS** (See also Climate)

As already mentioned, early season (December) is a
gamble. There has been a lack of early snow in recent years,
so at this time of year it is best to aim high and go to a summer

247

**S** ski resort where you are sure of glacier skiing. The drawback is that it might be cold and there's a certain amount of skiing over rocks which is not necessarily the best introduction to winter sports holidays.

In January the snow is usually crisp, dry and a dream to ski. But it can be bitterly cold. Again not a good choice for novices. February would be the best if it weren't for school holidays (see HOLIDAYS). March is warmer, sunnier and altogether more pleasant. However, the snow can get patchy on the runs leading down to the village, and sunshine combined with fewer snowfalls and overnight freezing results in some icy starts. This is not always the case, however: metres of powder snow can fall in spring. April is more risky and you should select a high-altitude resort for best conditions.

Pistes are generally hard-packed, as they are bashed down by skiers or special machines as soon as the fresh snow falls. Off-piste refers to areas that are not bashed by machines or skied regularly. You shouldn't leap into this great white wilderness unless you're an expert. Even then, you should make sure you know the mountain, otherwise you can never tell what may be lurking under the snow or round the next bend. If you are at all unfamiliar with the terrain, take an instructor or guide. In particular, take special notice of avalanche warnings (yellow and black checked flag). Don't go off piste on a glacier; there is a danger of crevasses, large cracks in the ice sometimes concealed by snow. Remember that if anything should go wrong, patrols are irregular or non-existent away from the pistes. Snow and the mountains may appear innocuous, but they claim many lives every year.

You will find different types of snow on or off piste. If you thought they were simply white flakes that fell out of the sky, you'll discover differently when skiing.

**Powder snow.** The proverbial skier's dream: crystals of light, dry snow that cannot be formed into a ball. Off piste you float through it; freshly packed down on piste it is easy to glide over. Not all fresh snow is powder. If the weather is warmer, big, wet flakes will fall and that's not the same thing

at all. Always beware of avalanches off piste after a heavy **S**
snowfall.

**Hardpack.** This common piste condition results from snow
which has been compressed over a few days without a
snowfall. Moguls (bumps) form and icy or even bare patches
develop should it not snow again for a while.

**Porridge** is snow which has been chopped up by skiers. It
can refer to fresh snow which has been skied over without
being bashed by the piste machines. Or, in spring when it is
warmer and the sun shines, surface snow softens and the
pistes get slushy—just like pea soup.

**Spring snow** (also known as corn snow). This is lovely to ski,
especially off piste. Smooth, wet snow freezes overnight, and
first thing in the morning the texture is like granulated sugar.
When the surface has just softened it develops a sheen. This
snow is very easy to ski but sadly short-lived. By lunchtime it
has got too slushy, but is good to try monoskiing in.

**Windslab** is an off-piste condition caused by wind blowing
powder snow and depositing it in the lee of the mountain,
packing it down hard and seemingly unbreakable. It is very
dangerous, as great chunks break away in slab avalanches.

**Breakable crust.** This happens to fresh snow off piste when
the surface melts during the day and freezes overnight. It is
very difficult to ski over.

## TOURIST INFORMATION OFFICE                                    **T**

The Austrian National Tourist Office, 30 St. George Street,
London W1R OAL, tel. (01) 629 0461, will provide brochures
and give advice, but does not book holidays. If telephoning,
have patience. Lines are very busy and you may have to
hang on for a reply. The London office will provide details of
the local tourist office in your selected ski resort.

## SOME USEFUL EXPRESSIONS

### Equipment

| | |
|---|---|
| I'd like to hire/buy ... | Ich würde gerne ... mieten/kaufen. |
| ski boots | Skischuhe |
| ski poles | Skistöcke |
| skis | Skier |
| What length poles/skis should I have? | Wie lang sollten meine Stöcke/Skier sein? |
| Can you adjust the bindings? | Könnten Sie bitte meine Bindungen einstellen? |
| Can you wax my skis? | Könnten Sie bitte meine Skier wachsen? |
| Can you sharpen the edges? | Könnten Sie bitte meine Kanten schärfen? |
| I am a ... | Ich bin ein ... |
| beginner | Anfänger |
| intermediate skier | fortgeschrittener Skiläufer |
| advanced skier | guter Skiläufer |
| I weigh ... kilos. | Ich wiege ... Kilo |
| My shoe size is ... | Meine Schuhgrösse ist ... |

| British | 4 | 5 | 6 | 6½ | 7 | 8 | 8½ | 9 | 9½ | 10 | 11 |
|---|---|---|---|---|---|---|---|---|---|---|---|
| Continental | 37 | 38 | 39 | 40 | 41 | 42 | 43 | 43 | 44 | 44 | 45 |

| | |
|---|---|
| These boots are ... | Diese Schuhe sind ... |
| too big/too small | zu gross/zu klein |
| uncomfortable | unbequem |
| Do you have any rear-entry boots? | Haben Sie Schuhe mit Hintereinstieg? |

### Problems

| | |
|---|---|
| My skis are too long/too short. | Meine Skier sind zu lang/zu kurz. |
| My ski/pole has broken. | Mein Ski/Stock ist kaputt. |
| My bindings are too loose/too tight. | Meine Bindungen sind zu locker/zu fest. |
| The clasp on my boot is broken. | Die Schnalle an meinem Schuh ist kaputt. |
| My boots hurt me. | Meine Schuhe tun mir weh. |

## Clothing and accessories

| | |
|---|---|
| *bumbag* | Lendentasche |
| *gloves* | Handschuhe |
| *goggles* | Schneebrille |
| *hat* | Mütze |
| *headband* | Stirnband |
| *jacket* | Jacke |
| *mittens* | Fäustlinge |
| *one-piece suit* | Overall |
| *polo-neck sweater* | Rollkragen-Pullover |
| *rucksack* | Rucksack |
| *ski suit* | Skianzug |
| *ski trousers* | Skihose |
| *socks* | Socken |
| *sun glasses* | Sonnenbrille |

and don't forget:

| | |
|---|---|
| *lip salve* | Lippenpomade |
| *sun cream* | Sonnencreme |

## Lifts and lift passes

| | |
|---|---|
| *I'd like a ...* | Ich hätte gerne einen ... |
| *lift pass* | Skipass |
|   *day* |   Tag |
|   *season* |   Saison |
|   *week* |   Woche |
| *I'd like a book of ... lift coupons.* | Ich hätte gerne einen Block mit ... Lift-Coupons. |
|   *ten/twenty/thirty* |   zehn/zwanzig/dreissig |
| *Do I need a photo?* | Brauche ich ein Foto? |
| *Could I have a lift-pass holder?* | Hätten Sie eine Hülle für den Skipass? |
| *cable car* | Luftseilbahn |
| *chair lift* | Sessellift |
| *drag lift* | Schlepplift |
| *gondola* | Gondel |
| *Where's the end of the queue?* | Wo ist das Ende der Schlange? |
| *Can I have a piste map, please?* | Könnte ich bitte einen Plan der Pisten haben? |

## On the piste

| Where are the nursery slopes? | Wo sind die Anfängerhügel? |
| Which is the easiest way down? | Welches ist die einfachste Abfahrt |
| It's a(n) ... run. | Es ist eine ... Abfahrt. |
| easy/difficult | leichte/schwere |
| gentle/steep | flache/steile |
| green (very easy) | grüne (sehr leichte) |
| blue (easy) | blaue (leichte) |
| red (intermediate) | rote (mittelschwere) |
| black (difficult) | schwarze (schwere) |
| The piste is closed. | Die Piste ist gesperrt. |
| The piste is very icy. | Die Piste ist sehr eisig. |
| ... snow | ... Schnee |
| deep | Tiefschnee |
| powder | Pulverschnee |
| sticky | Pappschnee |
| mogul (bump) | Buckel |
| rock | Stein |
| tree | Baum |
| Watch out! | Achtung!/Vorsicht! |

## Ski school

| I'd like some skiing lessons. | Ich hätte gerne Skistunden. |
| group/private | Gruppe/privat |
| Is there an English-speaking instructor? | Gibt es einen englisch-sprachigen Lehrer? |

If the answer is no, then the following will come in handy:

| snowplough | Schneepflug |
| stem christie | Stemm-Christiania |
| parallel turn | Parallelschwung |
| downhill ski | Talski |
| uphill ski | Bergski |
| Weight on the downhill ski. | Talski belasten. |
| Bend your knees. | In die Knie gehen. |
| Tuck your bottom in. | Hüften nach vorne. |
| Lean forward. | In die Vorlage. |
| Traverse the piste ... | Die Piste ... überqueren. |

| slowly | langsam |
|--------|---------|
| faster | schneller |
| *Slow down.* | Bremsen. |
| *Stop.* | Stop. |
| *Follow me.* | Folgen Sie mir. |
| *Shoulders towards the valley.* | Schultern talwärts. |
| *Up-down-up.* | Hoch-tief-hoch. |
| *Unweight your skis.* | Skier entlasten. |
| *Transfer your weight now.* | Verlagern Sie jetzt Ihr Gewicht. |
| *left/right* | links/rechts |
| *herring bone* | Grätenschritt |
| *side-stepping* | Treppenschritt |
| *side-slipping* | seitwärts rutschen |
| *Poles behind you.* | Stöcke nach hinten. |
| *Edge/Flatten your skis.* | Kanten belasten/Skier laufen lassen. |
| *Keep your skis parallel.* | Halten Sie Ihre Skier parallel. |
| *Put your skis together.* | Halten Sie die Skier zusammen. |
| *Keep the skis flat and evenly weighted.* | Skier laufen lassen und beide gleich belasten. |

## Emergencies

| *I can't move my ...* | Ich kann mein(en) ... nicht bewegen. |
|--------|---------|
| *My ... hurts.* | Mein ... tut weh. |
| back | Rücken |
| finger | Finger |
| knee | Knie |
| neck | Hals |
| wrist | Handgelenk |
| *I've pulled a muscle.* | Ich habe einen Muskel gezerrt. |
| *Please get help.* | Bitte holen Sie Hilfe. |
| *Don't move.* | Bewegen Sie sich nicht. |
| *avalanche danger* | Lawinengefahr |
| *rescue service* | Rettungsdienst |

# INDEX

An asterisk (*) next to a page number indicates a map reference. Where there is more than one set of page references, the one in bold type refers to the main entry. For index to Practical Information, see page 227.